# WORDS MADE OF SILK

BY

## JEAN-YVES SOLINGA

Special Limited Edition

# FIRST EDITION

Little Red Tree Publishing, LLC,
635 Ocean Avenue, New London, CT 06320

Manufactured in USA

First Edition 2011

Cover and Book Design:
Michael John Linnard, MCSD and Elaine Mills

Cover photographs are public domain images but altered to reflect tones of Majorelle Blue.

Library of Congress Cataloging-in-Publication Data:

Solinga, Jean-Yves
  Words made of Silk / by Jean-Yves Solinga. -- 1st ed.
     p. cm.
  Includes glossary.
  Includes index.
  ISBN-13: 978-0-935656-01-2 (pbk. : alk. paper)
  I. Title.
  PS3619.O4326C55 2008
  811'.6--dc22
                              2011016251

Little Red Tree Publishing, LLC
635 Ocean Avenue,
New London, CT 06320
website: www.littleredtree.com

# CONTENTS

**CHAPTER III**          **Poems of New England isolation:**

# FOREWORD

It is without doubt a privilege for Little Red Tree Publishing, of New London, to once again publish a new collection of poems by Jean-Yves Solinga called **Words Made of Silk**.

As I read Jean-Yves' poems for this collection, I was reminded of my initial impression when reviewing his first manuscript: that here before me is, "...a poet with an effortless ability to use language, conveying myriad emotions, that create an ambience of mellifluous subtlety with immense depth...." It was true then and remains so today.

He continues to eschew more traditional forms, without appearing to be affected or pretentious. Rather it is immanent and that his expansive vision and narrative voice as a poet goes further and purposefully plays with the very notion of poetry to the extent of attenuation: to the anti-poetic.

This should not be viewed as undermining the harmony or sonority of the literary genre but a concrete and purposeful attempt to tease out every last drop of meaning and didactic possibility from every word. Essentially Jean-Yves is attempting to produce a cognitive dissonance, to dislocate or interrupt the traditional notions of poetic language in the service of the greater goal of communicating a deeper meaning. It is by definition avant-garde and paves the way into unexplored regions of personal creativity and new ways of perceiving the reality we all experience.

This aesthetic anti-poetic underpinning is not in any sense without purpose and there is a self-evident awareness of the potential conflict with his own natural sense of mellifluous prose. Therefore, one will be able to detect the conflict and duality within the contrasting subject matter of the poems in this book. Jean-Yves floats with consummate ease between the real tragic consequences of egregious acts of inhumanity, and the ineffable and ethereal vapors of sensual erotic sensibilities: an innate, subliminal yet synergic tour de force.

The very title of this book, **Words made of Silk**, is in many ways a window into the poetic process and mind of Jean-Yves, wherein he is trying to use the physical attributes of silk as a metaphor for the infinite emotional and flexible capacity of words. I was very glad to find a suitable set of images that in my view captured the essence of the color and fluidity that was suggested by the title in a meaningful manner.

Therefore, I present this beautiful book from a poet who has lived a life of academic and cultural duality. A remarkable book of poetry that must be read by all those interested in a singularly unique view of life that may re-define in your mind the capacity of poetry to be what it was always meant to be.

Michael Linnard, CEO
Little Red Tree Publishing,
New London, CT 2011

# PREFACE

Writing, unless you want to keep all existing forms of your work in a back room closet, is meant for some conceivable public consumption. This step opens art to outside evaluation, demand, critique and sometimes, rewards. And so the question: "Writing poetry in an increasingly fast technological world...Why?" Well, my standard and very personal answer is, "In order to buy a Maserati." But more practically: I believe the poet, through the natural density of the genre, can make compact statements and point to, if that is what he wants, to some vision of beauty and or ethical behavior.

Taste in things artistic can be mercilessly personal. We know of some of the giants of the past: composers, painters, novelists, who could not put on their operas, give away their paintings, find a publisher. There is, of course, the anecdotal retort about the *Mona Lisa*: "She's not that great of a painting!"

And yet we have the musician in his garage; or the English teacher on his weekends; tirelessly composing and artistically trying to capture that ethereal mood through the winter branches.

Which brings us to my reason to continue writing: I am simply compelled to write. And yes, in the final analysis, I do write hopefully for that eventual someone in whom I can find some artistic approval and with whom and for whom I can recreate an approving nod in front of some truth or some hidden beauty.

Regarding an increasingly important topic, unrelated to the quality or substance of any poetry, is the issue of the nature of transmission of the written word in an ever changing technology.

The formats, and choices of formats, are becoming an integral part of success or survival. In this brave new world of astonishing access of anything to anyone, the discrimination and appreciation of degrees in the quality and effort of various works seem to numb the mind. It seems to me that everyone and no-one has a vote in the anonymous internet cloud. I am reminded of that scene in Fahrenheit 451 when the whole country is waiting, on live television from her kitchen, for the opinion of a bored housewife. What is the precise worth of that evaluation? The odds of my getting that Maserati are at stake here!

Fortunately, there are still those precious or important moments that I personally continue to choose to stop in space and time: The memory of a glance. A particularly insidious injustice that needs to be shamed. And so, each artist, any artist takes her or his place in front of the wall and inserts a little piece of polished Majorelle blue stone into the greater mosaic.

*Words Made Of Silk* is the fifth book of poetry that Michael Linnard of Little Red Tree Publishing and I have produced and I once more want to deeply acknowledge his professionalism and personal friendship.

My family and circle of friends have given me more than my share of what can still be good and just in our individual lives in spite of too many examples to the contrary in our world. And on this note, there are few moments more symbolic of our faith in humanity than our children having children. To that end, two poems in this collection are dedicated to my grandchildren.

Jean-Yves Vincent Solinga
Gales Ferry
Spring 2011

# INTRODUCTION

**A year's worth....**

These poems are pulled toward two very contrasting poles: hard reality and vaporous lyricism. At times, the fluctuation between the thematic in the chapter listing of the poems is extreme. The split in my state of mind is not new but it has evolved into immediacy: into an urgency in the more graphic expression of some of these multiple realities. A world where we cherish living and loving, where we can witness the biological beauty of the earth and yet see loved ones disappear and the fragile environment constantly threatened.

It was the split of my cultural world that divided my poetic world in *Clair-Obscur of the Soul.* And I still feel the need to explore the inner working of things: the more complicated truths behind the events, the people, the laws, the inventions that touch us: "Dream Sequence: The Silent Man," "Dream Sequence Four: The Lost Man Of Mankind," "Just Doing His Job."

There are morally compromised relationships; Faustian bargains that we would rather keep hidden in order to sleep more soundly at night. For example, many of the basic elements needed for the function of our modern equipment come from troubled or impoverished areas of the world. We have, in addition, otherwise mild mannered, God fearing social acquaintances who work on unethical products or behave unethically: "Just Doing His Job," "Aging Executive With Benefits." It would be so much more comfortable to have poetry evolve only in a safe, filtered atmosphere; but that has never been the case.

This oscillation in the thematic of my poems, found in the softness of the colored reconstructions of past memories, or the quasi anti-poetic of genocidal history, could have been a major dilemma in the determination of chapter headings and subdivisions. Should I have strived for a balance in the number of respective entries between these two worlds of lyricism and hard reality?

It occurred to me that, instead of trying to reconcile these opposite tendencies in the order of the poems, I could, with just some slight alterations use the chronological inception of each poem. This results in a real life exemplar of artistic rumination. And so, this explains the subheading of this introduction: "A year's worth...."

There is indeed about a year's time between "Of Beautiful Curves And Economic Decrepitude" and "Magical Dust" and the result is truly a sort of artistic journal.

This book turned into a photographic negative plate, a concrete compilation of the effects of the inside and outside worlds on the mind: the gratuitous vagaries of remembrance. The unsolicited intrusions of the past. The unwanted or unstoppable reflections on all of that baggage: Precious. Cumbersome. Irretrievable.

I have taken some liberties with what would be more traditionally considered topics of the poetic genre. I was even tempted to compile a chapter under the heading: *anti-poems* or *anti-poetry*. This, akin to what some of the poets of the *Theatre of the Absurd*, such as Eugène Ionesco and Samuel Becket did in their attempts at dramatic plays that purposefully devalued speech. That is, deconstruct words to their lowest communicative level in order to parse out their potential inner power in political, militaristic propaganda, or interpersonal role in lies and truth: "The Bald Soprano," "Rhinocéros," "Waiting for Godot."

This is again the case in poems like "If" (About a grammatical rule in French), "Literary Theories at the personal level" (About the very academic concept of the 'signified' and the 'signifier' in the New Critic.) or "Of Revolution And Luck" (About the physical distance between Great Britain and America that allowed the fighting to be more benign and therefore the repression less intense as compared to the one in France where revolutionaries were surrounded within miles by multiple fearful monarchies). "Rorschach Nation" (How to interpret the original intent of the United States Constitution? What do we mean by loaded signifier words like: woman, disagreement, allegiance?

But the relationship between the poet and his art [Yes, indeed, his Muse] is still paramount to me. It is still at the intersection of things untouchable that the human mind redeems itself even if it is at times guilty of reprehensible actions: "African Harmony" versus "The Flower And The Butterfly." The unfiltered evil of genocide of the former and the images of tenderness in nature. Flaubert did not need to have a beautiful subject; but rather the goal of beautiful descriptions. Indeed, privileged is he who, in that half world between sleep and full consciousness, can still hear the last words of his muse as she hides in the half shadows at the foot of his bed: "The Painting," "Magical Ink," "Ghost," "Words Made Of Silk," and "The Gentle Princess."

The recurring theme and presence of silk opened a lyrical world at the crossroad of the organic and transcendental. There is indeed in that substance the multiplicity of life after animal life: sensuality of touch and sight as captured by the book cover and associated poems.

Some poems have a definite sharp political edge and are meant to cause some well-deserved discomfort: "High Tech Machines And Killings," "African Harmony," "Just Doing His Job," "Of Children's Games And Full Metal Jackets," "Live Television Feed From The Crucifixion" or even "Bordeaux-like Wines."

Physical or emotional 'isolation' (as mentioned in the title to Chapter III) makes the mirror a metaphor for a window on the inner and outer worlds: Montaigne retreated to his tower in order to reflect on himself and in his thoughts he found pieces of mankind. Adding an extra layering of interpretation, I have plainly indicated the leitmotifs in some of the themes of previously published ones: "A Glorious Moment," "Magical dust," "Dreams of Blue Silk," for instance.

As usual, I do not tie my poetry directly or obviously to my life. Firstly, because my esthetic is that art can stand on its own: real or fictional. Secondly, because the use of pastiche, or assemblage of a collage of fiction on the surface of reality, give the artist unbridled freedom: especially in my dream sequence poems.

But some topics are essentially inspired from personal or political background as should be evident to the reader. For example, "Flattened Memories" is about my mother, sister and brother (During World War I for my mother and then World War II for all three). "Same Street... Different Worlds" is about a dear friend who had just lost his wife while we, unknowingly, were having a wonderful Thanksgiving dinner. These are the types of antithetical worlds that poetry distils so well.

And under the heading that mankind, in spite of all the horrors that can befall it, is capable of symbols of hope, "Fragile Letters" is dedicated to my first grandchild, Noëlle, and "The Symbol Of Things Good" to Luc my first grandson.

Jean-Yves Vincent Solinga
Gales Ferry, Connecticut
Spring 2011

# CHAPTER I

# LESSONS AMONG THE CITY

Poems started around and in an urban setting: constant intrusion of reality while restarting interrupted stream of lyricism.

# DREAMS OF BLUE SILK

Sharp diagonal waves in shades of sparkling blues
Splendid hidden bodily fluidity...

Linking under animal secretions
Human appetites.

From humble birth as simple mucus,
A natural emission containing their cocooned tomorrows.

Yet noble corporal covering
Witness to so many midnight whispers.

Divinity of clothing worthy of the most secretive tabernacles
Permitted to touch the most precious of quivering bare folds of flesh.

A visceral slime spun into the privileged veil
For simmering lubricities.

Binding intimate memories in strands from unfurled cocoons
Wrapping in bundles of moments
Vanished glances and embraces.

Animal film undulating over feminine curves
Creating shimmering mysteries
Away from envious glances.

Like all dreams, like all envies
Like all human wisdom made of unrepentant mortal sins

She was... in the angular spread of her body
The incarnation of the very earthly trinities
That are...
Youth, Love and Possession.
Tenderness. Resilience and Beauty.

# OF BEAUTIFUL CURVES AND ECONOMIC DECREPITUDE

Ironic.
Ironic that these exquisite statues would be in the lower level.
Their weight. Their heft. Their solidity maybe.

No matter.
Quietly and gently year after year
They carry the meaning of artistic desire
In the plasticity of their folds of marble.

Long muscles captured long ago in the dust of Antiquity.
The genesis of a smile stopped in mid sigh by the chisel.

This young woman is now on the same level
As the majestic granite of majestic organic mountains.

Dimples in the flesh of the discus thrower,
Stopped in its sweaty effort, that now stops the eye of the tourist.

All this beauty rendered that much more beautiful
By the ensuing disintegration of style:
The Middle Ages seemingly afraid of the instrumentality
Behind the drive and splendor of the beginnings of life
Found in the human body.

Who were these men that roamed these ancient cities
Endowed with the critical mass of all great artistry:

That of extraordinary talent and unfettered courage?

Almost an afterthought this descent into the Museum:
Marble staircase of a dated imposing style
Of wealthy late nineteenth century construction.

In a long drab hall way... a statuary that tells the story
Of the spreading of the molecules of Greek culture.

Such as early roman attempts at imitating this art:

Mastering it... but not replacing it.
The Greeks had found it and are still keeping it in these stones
Still rounded with the carnal sensuality that distills envy.

Eternal understated female pubescence that speaks of the future.
The proud authenticity of male nudity still exuding solar light.

They had reached that place that few cultures contemplate:

Like the composer at three in the morning.
The painter waking up in front of his still glistening work.

The writer rereading the first act, scene one
In the wrinkled pages of last night.

Did these Greek artists know that they had in front of them
The solid representation...
            ... so far back... and so originally...

That gives homage, in space and time,
To what Life can envision in representing the essences of itself.

*Reflections gorgeous Greek sculptures dating hundreds of years BC and the sad status of Greece's finances in the early twenty first century.*

## "BORDEAUX-LIKE WINES"

Pseudo-medical studies. Quasi-good cheese.
Nearly-tasty bread. Almost-pleasant first date.

A new universe of Asymptotes has opened up all around us:
Coming close to the thing, the real thing.
The thing that would be our goal, if it were our goal,

But... never touching it. Never reaching it.
Coming maddeningly close to it.

What a great achievement. What a way to live.

Yes! Have everything, anything... but the real thing!
We only sell English-like beers.

Sadly perusing the pages of the wine list:
Knowing the real liquid is readily available.

Mumbling: "At least it's not religious intolerance."


*Trendy big city restaurant wine list entry 2010: "Bordeaux-like wines."*

*At least, it's not "Freedom fries."*

# THINKING TOO MUCH

He had done so well.
Diplomas in hand and life on proper track.

Better New England schools and MD suffix.
You could not write a sweeter script of accomplishments.
Doing what he liked and doing it well.

His life had found the equitable center:
Scientific certainty and aptitude,
Along with emotional stability of relationships.

Respected by colleagues and toasted by friends...
　　　... Until that endless ride home to the suburbs.

Coming home, shaken by his unbridled thoughts:
With a slight taste of bile and disgust toward his arrogance.

With more sensitivity in his knowledge of himself and others.
With a wiser reverence for what he knew... And didn't.
For what he had felt... And should have.

———————————————

He had that afternoon done
What he did: masterfully and repeatedly.
Well and professionally.

He had efficiently and properly
With protocol and coolly...
... Chosen a fertilized egg... For a couple.
And sent that bundle of cells to be inseminated.

Repetition and self-assuredness had jaded him.
The tip of his pipette was an extension of his training:
No more. No less.

Years of self-absorbency and learning
Had autoclaved any divine source in his actions:
Any definition was firmly based in his own determination.

But that night,
As he has laid wracked with insomnia next to his wife,

He took in the full meaning of what he had done,
For a nameless couple and their lineage.

In the sterility of his laboratory... In the quiet of that afternoon.


*In praise of sciences at the service of humanity.*

# SOMETIMES... MIRAGES ARE REAL

She sometimes would be there... on the other side of the glass
When, stupefied, he believed seeing her again
Surrounded by the luminous patina of remembrance.

She would appear to him made of beautiful anonymous curves
Climbing a nameless urban staircase.

She would exist once more in the randomness of Time
Through an ambivalent laughter,
With virile feminine undercurrents,

Escaping from rounded lips calling back to
The corporal desires gone now in the desert of absence.

Everything had evolved into vapor,
Tears and illusions. Everything.

She had, at times, become perfumed molecules
Made of Mediterranean petals evaporating from anonymous
Bodies in the overheated summers in Provençal creeks.

He would at times recognize her in the familiar sound
From sighs overheard through much too thin hotel walls.

She would often incarnate the fictitious and precious
Screen images of movies discussed among friends
In the mundane noise of coffee houses.

Was she this invisible voice coming from the lower level?
Was she, in the improbable setting of a hallway,
Going to answer to this first name with such rare overtones?

Everything and nothings. Things and people.
Common objects and their frustrating daily reflections

That would too quickly glide off his soul and body...
... And he, not being able to stop it.

She thus had learned to easily reside
In the free spaces of his thoughts and dreams:
Followed by recurring consciousness full of regrets.

She had managed to live just long enough...
... In this privileged space...
... The one between sleep and the first gulp of coffee,

In order to finally disappear in the totality of things.

He had started to appreciate the value of lost presences
That had gone into the space of other lives, where...

Everything would continue to be...
Vapor, tears and illusions. Everything.

Except... the pain.

# DES FOIS, LES MIRAGES SONT VRAIS

Elle était des fois, là... de l'autre côté d'une vitre
Quand, stupéfait, il croyait la revoir
Faite de la patine lumineuse de souvenirs.

Il se prenait à la voir construite de belles hanches anonymes
Montant des escaliers urbains sans nom.

Elle existait de nouveau, à n'importe quel moment,
À travers un rire ambivalent au sous ton féminin viril
S'échappant de lèvres aux rondeurs rappelant
Le charnel des désirs évaporés dans le désert de l'absence.

Tout s'était transformé en vapeur,
Pleurs et illusion. Tout.

Elle était aussi, par moments, devenue molécules parfumées
Aux pétales méditerranéens s'évaporant des peaux anonymes
D'étés surchauffés sur les galets d'une calanque.

Il l'a reconnaissait parfois à travers un son familier
Basé sur un soupir deviné à travers une trop fine cloison d'hôtel.

Elle incarnait souvent les images fictives et précieuses
De films discutés entre amis dans le bruit ordinaire d'un café.

Était-elle cette voix invisible sur le palier d'en bas ?
Allait-elle, dans le hasard d'un couloir,
Répondre à ce prénom similaire au sien, pourtant si rare ?

Des tous et des riens. Des choses et des personnes.
Des objets banals et leurs réflexions quotidiennes frustrantes
Glissant trop vite sur son âme et son corps...
... Ne pouvant les arrêter.

Elle avait appris à évoluer pourtant si aisément
Dans la liberté de ses pensées et rêves :
Suivis de réveilles récurrents remplis de déception.

Elle arrivait à vivre juste assez longtemps...
... Dans cet espace privilégié...
... Celui entre le sommeil et la première gorgée de café,

Pour finalement disparaître dans la pureté chimérique de tout cela.

Il avait commencé à apprendre la valeur des présences disparues
Dans l'ailleurs des autres vies, là... où...

Tout ne continuait à être...
Que vapeur, pleurs et illusion. Tout.

Sauf... la peine.

# GHOST

She will be... She will have been... That much more present
... As a result of her very absence.

Having filled the smallest corners of his life,
She will have become that very shadow
That one can discern among other shadows.

Shiny apparition on the oblique surrealism
Discovered on a window full of summer.

The immodest daydream that one expects
At the foot of the bed in the darkness of insomnia.

The feminine voice with persistent intimate virile tonalities
That one seems to hear from a Spirit in translucent veils.

Invention made of daily fantasies
Constructed between shopping for bread and a cup of coffee.

She is still here... Present... And for always.
Yet long gone and forever.

*Reflection on mankind's consciousness of the ephemeral nature of Things
thus making its struggle against loss one of his greatest worth.*

*From the French, La revenante,*

## LA REVENANTE

Elle sera... elle aura été... d'autant plus présente
... Par son absence.

Ayant rempli les plus petits recoins de sa vie,
Elle sera devenue l'ombre que l'on pense deviner sur les ombres.

L'apparition glissant sur l'oblique surréaliste d'une fenêtre d'été.
La chimère impudique que l'on attend au pied du lit
Dans le noir d'une insomnie.

La voix féminine aux intonations viriles encore intimes
Que l'on croit entendre d'un esprit aux voiles translucides.

Construction faite de phantasmes quotidiens
Entre la boulangerie et la tasse de café.

Présente... là... et pour toujours.
Pourtant disparue depuis longtemps et pour jamais.


*Les penseurs ont souvent vu, dans l'existence de la conscience des choses chez l'homme, la beauté de sa plus grande valeur et la source de la générosité de son plus grand combat.*

# A GLORIOUS MOMENT

Ah! To die the death of the excesses of some artists...

The one unseen around a sharp corner of life.
The unheard explosion of a vital cerebral vein.
The sudden stop of electrical cardiac impulse.
The final intake of breath of over abused lungs...

... On the way back to the wrinkled sheets,
The steamy curves and languorous eyes,
Unfinished embraces and eternal lubricity,

Waiting on the landscape of envies
In the nuptial cottony shadows.

---

To die full of flowing energy:

Looking with hunger and thirst
Upon the most important moments of our existence...
... The next few minutes.

To die with an illusionary emptied glance
On the harsher realities outside of the Temple.

Gorging oneself on the single-minded satiated sensualities
... Of living... Living.

Instead of... The stoicism and wisdom,
Acquired with age, painful decrepitude and sorrows,

That sadly make us accept the unacceptable.

*Reflection on Jim Morrison's grave and the poem "To Live and Die in Paris" in*
Clair-Obscur of the Soul (2008).

*"City of light, city of night*
*Where are you Jim? Talk to us from Père Lachaise...*
*Did that work for you?"*

# MOSAIC PIECES

Flakey explosions of buttery pastry crust.
Aromatic vapors from Italian coffee machines.

Wicker chairs under noble plane trees.
Shy lights from sidewalk incandescence
Giving greenish blue sheen to phantom leaves.

Nervous mosquito noises
From mopeds mounted by youths
In search of sleepless nights.

Envied conversations from the intimacy of tables:
Tales of budding illicit office romance
And spontaneous plans for the evening.

Hints of neoclassical freezes above majestic doorways.
Massive wooden doors witness to street revolutions,

Followed by anxiety that even magical hours are not eternal.

The sensual intelligence of the banter will come to an end.
The Métro will arrive and she'll be gone.

*Paris*

# JUST DOING HIS JOB

In an appropriate cliché: he was a God fearing man.
Known for his routines and peculiar habits.

Smallish Middle American city made of traditional mores:
Sprinkled with Baseball practice at Little League park.
Fund raising for local bird sanctuary and abandoned animals.

Heavy unattractive plastic glasses and non-coordinating socks:
Geekish leftovers from scientific university track.

Rockwellian scripted life:
In love with shy girl in Algebra Two class,
Producing a logically statistical three children.

Ice cream at Fred's on Fridays.
Second pew from the left on Sundays.

Dependable family provider and all around good neighbor:
Punctual employee and ready plumbing tools for emergencies.

Follower of Biblical strictures and State driving code:
A moral man living in the gentle breezes of quietude.

A man who could... Should... Surely must have
Closed his eyes peacefully on that late day, late in his life.

Litany of accomplishments: sacred and secular.
Glowing obituary and heartfelt accolades for widow.

A good productive life if you will...
Although... He had, during the War, worked silently, diligently
To perfect the nozzle efficiency and control...

... On the flamethrower...

*The reader can substitute any of the scientific 'innovations' to the arsenal of warfare. Such things as: anti-personnel mines, cluster bombs, timing device on thermonuclear bombs, Napalm, the machine gun, poison gas etc...*

*To the anti-war song by Alain Souchon: "C'est comme vous voulez."*

# CONTRADICTORY THOUGHTS

A stranded extraterrestrial colony would not last without it.
Preciously recycling any production of it: Sweat and other
things.

On other worlds... Of three Moons and two Suns,
With fine reddish powder of oxidized iron all around,
The cosmonauts would be left drinking
Chemically filtered bodily fluids.

Normally existing liquid water,
A stupefying chemical improbability,
Seems to be an under appreciated metaphor
For Mankind's continued existence.

Feeling thus a little guilty at the damning thoughts,
Upon another three inches of water seeping under the stairs.

Considering the absolutely marvelous aspects of this substance
As it invades sleepless nights.

Seeing humanity as but a rudderless bobbing entity
On the arbitrary presence of watery worlds.

*Reflection at three in the morning while pushing water in the basement and
the scientific opinion that the very existence of this substance and its proper-
ties nears the miraculous.*

# EXISTENTIALISM AND MEDICAL SCHOOL

He had gone up these steps: Neo-classical columns on each side.
This, arguably, the world center of medical learning.

Late summer heat in his eyes, trepidation in his knees,
And years of study in this temple of medical prospecting.

One of the chosen. A sample of a selected few,
Destined to know things. Everything. Anything:
About things known and unknown.

Things of the flow of life,
And the insertion of impending destruction in the body flesh.
Of infectious diseases and powerful chemicals.

None of them yet useful in forestalling paternal death
And resulting disintegration of soul.

Now, an ex-religious person longing
For some sharpness, some stability of purpose.

Finding in the dividing lines of the orthodoxy of sciences
The needed clarity of vision and goals.

He finally sought strong fences between Good and Evil:
The ones anchored in walls around healthy bodies.

He had secreted in his being
Pieces of the traditional examples of youth.
Those made plank by plank by parental example.

He still could recognize in the haze of this past
Shades and shapes of the definition of the good:

Those of the standard currency of rewards on Earth
And down payments for Eternity.

Rewards based on this side of convenient reality
For those susceptible to Marxist criticism.

But these accolades had become useless to a soul
Blackened by the void of meaningful light.

He could not patronize in overtones made of platitudes
The Divine or its Divinities.

———————————————

Left, thus, searching for a source of Ethics
In a directionless travel with no rules of the road,

With equal anonymity in the great equation of existence
To our individual actions...
      Where doing or not doing,
            Right and left, receive the same disdain...
              As Good or Evil.

He found his definition in the solidarity
      Of his fight... Of our fight...

Against our collective mortal enemy:
The inevitability of our mortal destiny.

All this training, All these hours of preparation and dedication.
At the game of playing God:

But this time the marbles are for real pounds of flesh.


*Upon walking by Harvard's Medical School.*

*Ethics 101: Word in the news that ways could be increasingly available to correct, predict or undo future medical conditions in the embryo such as bi-sexuality, appearance etc... . What do we do with all this knowledge?*

*With literary thanks to Doctor Rieux of The Plague, by Albert Camus.*

*Nota Bene: The masculine voice could have been either gender.*

# LESSONS OF THE BASTILLE

Things learned and things symbolic.
Things change and stay the same.

Lessons learned. Repression and suspicion
From the gate keepers and people holding the keys.

Afraid of troublesome philosophers
And questioning intellectuals,

About unraveling the fragile threads of Social Contracts
And all around reciprocal political responsibilities.

Time comes to have these vaporous thoughts
Encircled by solid stones and mortar,
Or the modern media equivalent of imprisonment.

Stifle and quiet the spirits.

It didn't work then.
        It didn't work in between.
                It won't work now.

Patriotic laws to appeal to the knee-jerk patriotic
In any language or culture.
Squelching daring ideas of the daring and questioning kind.

All in all, favoring the non-critical herd and the lazy citizen.

Royal disapproval.  Senate speeches and scolding.
Reminding the individual of his duty:
Support the convenient way.  The traditional.

The delineated way:
Beware of these Others!

Long haired hippies,
Or revolutionaries Sans Culottes:
All the same in the annals of History.

Suffer the consequences if you defy:

Loss of friends.  Loss of security clearance.
Dishonorable discharge and no job recommendation.
Loss of bread or maybe... The occasional loss of life.

Back then the Bastille took them in.
Nixon's enemies list was fed by them.

The centuries follow each other in time.
The mistakes invariably come along for the ride.


*Upon reading an article on the Bastille: At least, some of the famous names
in the Bastille had sexual and drinking privileges.*

# FOURTEENTH

The baby had been given his starting number in life.
       He was apparently already behind.

It was only a number...
Cardinal, with no patronymic suffix.

No emotional or official compass
As to where from and where to.

But he had,
Under the sweltering heat of the Caribbean humidity,

The amputated limbs
And oozing infections,

He had,
With all his fingers and fed belly

He had...
His precious winning number,

In this life and death lottery.


*Inspired by a CNN report of the Haitian disaster of 2009 that babies were given anonymous numbers by medical staff.*

# OF SYMBOLIC FORETASTE OF THE NEW WORLD

Before the Statue in the New York Harbor,
Well before the doubly moist skyline on a September morning,

It had begun in the miniscule waves
In a bowl on a rocking ship.

Trying to hold on to disappearing impressions
Of wavy vaporous family faces

From steaming locomotive
Impatiently waiting at gare Saint Lazarre.

Metaphor of parental and linguistic loneliness
Seen in the stormy emptiness at dining room table.

Beginnings of encroaching foreign sounds
And weirdness of foreignness.

French waiter's friendly gesture
At introduction to the New World:
"Voilà ce qu'ils mangent au petit déjeuner."

Contradictory sensations of unrelated tastes:
Cardboard texture of grating surface
Mixed with overwhelming sugary milkiness.

Throwing oneself wholeheartedly
Into this Brave New World

Refusing in a fatalistic mood
Café crème and croissant au beurre.

Swallowing with knots of memories
The concrete evidence of change,

Not unlike those previously caused
By the sacrifice of a North African rooster.

*Author's first breakfast on the S.S. Flandre on the way to New York,*
*September 1959: a bowl of Kellogg's Corn Flakes with the rooster on the box.*
*"This is what THEY eat for breakfast."*

# OF SCRIBAL CORRUPTION AND INTOLERANCE

Subject without a verb.
Verb without a context.
Vernacular usage or figure of speech?

Local usage or imported terminology?
Was this meant to be erased or changed?

What to do with this extra word?
 Is this a stain or a letter on the parchment?

Which part is first? Where does this fragment apply?
Is this from the same document?

What if this is the ranting of an outsider's view?
          Was he a follower? Jealous? Ambitious?

These texts of venerable lineage
Of reputed divine extraction.
These concrete looks upon vaporous soul searching.

Cultural and sociological traces from upstream
Containing evidence of that peculiar human need:
For leadership. For clarity.

Written verbal miracle of survival from burnings...
Structural and human.
                Schisms... local and genocidal.
Organized mayhem and innovative tortures.

Religious updates. Rectifications and editorializing.
Paper trail of look into the fervor of mankind
As it reflects into the mirror of mankind.

Its place. Its purpose.
Its heading. Its fears and longing.

But what a leap of faith!
To accept the centuries of prejudice,

The inflicted pain and intolerance...

Over the literal meaning
The intended spirit
Or the accepted syntax... For universal wisdom.


*"Doubt is not a pleasant condition, but certainty is absurd." Voltaire.*

# WHAT WERE THE ODDS?

As casinos go, the Universe is merciless and evenhanded:
 It just does not care in that glass enclosed office.

Allowing for inconceivable number of participants:
 With few winners into the realm of consciousness.

Big Bangs and cosmological crap games
 Bringing us to that instant on the red velvet table top
  To that coastal town
   That unpretentious pier

And that intrusively nagging impression:

If that bird had never had the chance to fly over that pier,
 On that splendid summer day,

The universe, in its uneasy thermodynamic energy
 Would not have known... Or cared.

The sheets, of whitish reflections on the harbor waters,
Would, in their atomic simplicity,
Never have been associated with their impressionist cousins.

And no one would have known.

But it did happen.  And that was personally good.
 For that infinitesimal instant.
  In the momentary realization of a glance.

Adding to whatever that can conceivably mean,
 In the balance of Things.

# WRITING IN DARKNESS

Visions of Pre Genesis haunted his thoughts.
Of a time when the gods where elsewhere occupied.

A time of blackness when its very nuances had no name.
Of happiness and hope when both had no seeds or needs.

Of eye lashes when they had no form
To hold between them reflections of lubricity.

Things and couples were back
In the sterile aimless void
Of a merciless world with no merciful ending.

Nagging awareness that had always been there.
The afore knowledge that had often been acknowledged.

The premonition that had been ingrained
In the inherently impure complexity of the embrace.

But preparation had not made the moment slip easily by
As her presence so quietly did... from his arms.


*Of unhappy movies scripts.*

# THE SHADOW OF HER DOG

He knew, more than well, the lyrics:
Pedagogical voyeur and purveyor of feelings.

He had made his career
Out of pulling apart artistic peels.

One by one, he creatively had,
Intellectually and gently,
Dissected and scratched the most tender of seams.

Sensually rubbed between his fingers
The last molecules of the carnal dew from Others.

All of this with a professorial distance
That would present in intelligent synthesis
The plaintive wizardry of overarching chords.

He would scrupulously, during his classes,
Offer tastes of fragile luminous splendors
Similar to those of the most beautiful classic statues

That he would display during his scholarly hours
On the flat screens of walls and those, attentive, of the heart.

It happened, one day,
Waking up from his tranquilizing and tranquilized torpor,

Finding himself at that visceral level,
Where Truths would prefer to exist,

When he learned of the inadequacy of these feelings
Expressed, in his name, by others.

Without any resistance on their part,
The lyrics, now, stood out by the very weakness of their platitudes:

They had, without any fight, lost their potency
In front of the true, real and personal pain
That he was now living.


*"... Let me become*
*The shadow of your shadow*
*The shadow of your hand*
*The shadow of your dog*
*Don't ever leave me..."*

*In* "Ne me quitte pas" *by Jacques Brel*

# THIRD LEVEL... ON THE ALTAR

Local quarries offered their grayish yellow stones.
Forgotten masons and metal workers
Did their best imitations at pseudo Gothic lines.

Tenderly genial idea to plant chestnuts trees:
Giving plant-like memorial and respect
To human quirkiness for immortality.

Not a satisfactory end since it is the end.

But some modicum of victory over Things
In seeing, with a still living heart and active mind,

The splendidly irreverent stacking
Of dust returning to dust,

In quaint threesome pile,
On humble altar... In quiet chapel.


*The author's family has a Chapel in Marseille in the Saint Pierre Cemetery.*
*The author's mother and dog are already on the altar.*

# CHAPTER II

# UNCHARACTERISTIC PHILOSOPHY AMONG THE TREES AND BIRDS

Uncharacteristic philosophy among the trees and birds : An outdoor stream of consciousness affording some counter-balancing escapism from geopolitics.

## OF CHILDREN'S GAMES AND FULL METAL JACKETS

Snickering heard from sedate Graduate students.
Sly smirk from usually stern professor.

Derisory remarks of the pathetic world depicted.
Idiocy of behavior and insulting clownish attitudes portrayed.

This could not be. This should not be.
People and discourse cannot be so disjointed.

Scenes after absurd scenes of the theatre of the Absurd.

Title of unrelated value leaving viewer
Looking for entrance of the leading woman:
Any woman with no hair.

Non sequitur... Not answering simple questions.
Leaving audience clueless and characters blissfully satisfied.

Chief of the fire brigade
Disappointedly waiting to define himself in non-existing fires.

Ionesco must have decided, in a gratuitous moment,
To install these peculiar individuals between stage left and right

For no ulterior purpose.
No lesson. No future application.  No possible mirror to uphold.

If not... For the farcical behavior
Of stiff characters of flesh and blood
Both under their skins and on their suits

Men of political sustenance and girth.
Of geopolitical and military trust and vision.

Forthrightly and guiltlessly stating
The non-recollection of crucial moments

Starting in motion the mechanism
Sending forthrightly soldiers to kill and be killed
In an unshakable: "Senator, I cannot recall."

*Inspired by the lack of proportionality of the Congressional sanctions taken against Roger Clemens and previous testimonial lies and evasions from others with accompanying life and death issues.*

*And*

*The world of the illogical studied in literature class on Eugène Ionesco's the* Bald Soprano.

# HIGH TECH MACHINES AND KILLINGS

He particularly liked his view
     From the forty second floor:

With proper angle
     From his chair and time of year

He could see, all at once, one of his favorite trilogies:
     The antique silver picture frame of his precious daughters,

The reflections of the setting Sun on the Hudson,
     And the spire of the Empire State Building.

A truly blessed man
     In the mannerism of nineteenth Century parlance:

Rewarded by beautiful girls
     In best of New England Schools.

After years of blissful and protected upbringing
     In island of peace in East Side comfort.

A triple sign... There from his desk,
     From his God... to this God fearing man,

Of the worth of his soul
     In front of his maker and mankind.

Having found the seemingly prefect mixture
     Of things of the soul and technology.

Completely dependent on his umbilical links
     To latest electronics and stable family.

Giving respectively dual directions
     For fruitful mercantilism and personal happiness.
.....................................

He had looked once more
    Toward the omnipresent screen in his hands

For a market portfolio assessment...
    ... When his grasp loosened...

He could feel a deadly cold in his hands
    In the midst of a flashback.

Having read that morning
    About the genocidal sexual wars on the African Continent

Source of many of the rare earth elements
    Inside this machine... now made of blood.


*Prompted by news of the human cost in Central Africa for some of the raw materials of electronic technology.*

# OF COMIC BOOKS' ENDINGS

Young... With youth's ease for immediate satisfaction.

Yet... Background echoes of stern maternal tones
        About easy appearances. Respectability and responsibility.

Building brick by brick that emotional wall
That hits with the hardness of things that have endings.

Things and people filling rare moments
That should continue... But pass on.

Contradictory nature between the worth of things
And their apparent randomness.

Absence of hierarchy of their ultimate importance in our lives
Leaving us longing for the memories of accidental smells and tastes.

Discontinuity... Giving value to daily treasures.
Mosaic pieces of unrelated events.

Residual warmth distilled by time into nuggets that define living.
Nuggets too often buried in the mud of primordial youth.

Such as the first bite of favorite pastry after long church service.
        The last adventure of Tin Tin...
                Or... That unforeseen glance.

Injustices ingrained in the great calculus of things.
Built-in eternal disequilibrium.
Slyness of the thumb of the Absurd on the scale.

Early human appetites
        Threatened by the Puritanism of time and space.

Left hoping for other pastries to appear
Along with one more last minute happy ending...
        For a detective and his dog.

# THE EFFECT OF A BUTTERFLY

It surprised him.
Not the event... He had been expecting it.

No. Neither the pain:
He had been feeling it for a while,
Sharp and constant.

He had tried to live with it.
To surround himself in literary softness
In order to make things more pliable and tolerable.

No. No particular choc from this side
For such a Cosmopolitan man.

It was rather the surprising presence of this intellectual
nothingness.
An incalculable visceral emptiness.

The type that one keeps at arm's length during lifetime.
The type that one believes

To quietly being able to envision, as we wish,
In our philosophical corners.

The type, that under its abstract nature,
Bends more easily to our daily needs for survival.

A relatively benign void
In a relatively conceptual future.

A topic of discussion filling, between friends,
Smoky and animated evenings.

The void of philosophers and smart texts
That had offered him, quite pleasantly,
Moments of solidarity full of exaltation.

He would speak of it among his friends

All united against this adversary:

This unavoidable darkness
Against which they all had armed themselves.

They would throw, from the fortifications,
Rivers of scholastic disdain,

And later return home with their clear conscience
Intoxicated by cognac and bravery,

Knowing, all the while, that they had vaccinated their souls
Against the human virus: The one...

Of loving with too great a love
The too easy love of life.

No... this time it was total void.
The lack of all and of nothing.

Of this presence,
Already ghostlike in his life.

A cosmological emptiness,
Out of all humanistic proportion.

_____

Entering his home one night,
Glancing at the texts that he had read and written,

He realized the extent to which he envied these black letters
Which had been the source of so much luxurious discussions.

Now in the arid silence in this library
Surrounded by these bindings seemingly squeezed
To prevent their escape:

All of this provoked a shiver...
The real shiver... the Eternal shiver,

That represented this death...
His solitude...
Well before the event itself.


*The death of a Muse, by all account immortal: even if it is only in the form of a butterfly.*
*And,*
*The butterfly effect: A simple flutter of a butterfly's wings that, supposedly, can unleash a hurricane on the other side of the world.*

# AGING EXECUTIVE... WITH BENEFITS

His masterful business talent had formed an inverted image
In his miserable intimate life.

Three time loser at the altar of love,
Now living in the world of multiple alimonies,

He had lost all taste for the delusion of nuptials,
Happy endings and meaningful relationships,
With any fourth attempt at marital bliss.

Opting instead for long lasting affair with executive secretary
That he had to 'share with husband'

According to his flippant parlance and amoral rationalizing
In boozy male camaraderie and gatherings.

He had happily settled into an executive status
With 'privileges' on the same level as private parking spaces.

When a chance meeting and fifth floor hotel suite follow up
With former classmate... Happened in his life...

The way the sharp corners of life
Like to burst our bloated illusions.

A good friend, from his past, with potential and brain,
In his mostly all male law school and political tranquil days.

Feeling generous and emotionally obliged
He bedded that night and with efficiency the 'old girl'.

But he took that nagging feeling
Back to the East Coast and to his old ways:

That impression of having given the same jaded look
As that former girlfriend looked up...

Which seemed to have been the same glance
That his younger subservient subordinate
Had given him during their last time together.


*Another inspiration from the Universe of television.*

# THE GENTLE PRINCESS

They had met in the rich, complex, gentleness
That can sometimes encompass the landscape between youth and age.

One safely cushioned between inquisitive innocence and lasting
memories.

Devoted Knight and keeper of her secrets, she had allowed him
To watch over her susceptibilities and weaknesses.

With intimate flaws in her apparently flawless being
She entrusted him to personally protect her happiness.

He always knew that he, in turn, would be safe
There... in the chambers of her soul.

For this Princess had set a special place for him:
No matter where he was in this world
He could always find his way home.

Sheets of precious silk and cottony Egyptian drapes
Would guide his steps along the way
And soften the path back to her nuptial curves.

Warm gentle breezes over impressionistic fields
Would stream over his head directing his journey.

Perfumes made of the richest essences of exotic oils
Foretold him of her close presence.

She had become part of all parts of nature to him:
High Priestess of sensually clad muses
She even provoked simmering envies in the gaze of wise Druids.

She was the vibrating crimson fertile pistils in the garden.
The satiated shimmering leaves after the rain.

The pulsating wavelets kissing her toes
Hanging over the bank of their favorite pond.

She had become the embodiment of sighs
As he whispered over the fine hair on her nape
With the backdrop of crazed European traffic.

She was the voice and name so easily recognizable
Among all others in all other places and other languages.

He would have been no more surprised of her omnipresence
Than that of the stars, the moon and the sun:

She was and had been... just there.

Like all true princesses worthy of their true blue blood and status,
She was endowed with a generosity of heart,
A graceful demeanor and an intelligent sensitivity.

And thus, imperceptibly, almost silently, she made it felt
That time had come to be set free:

Princesses must live in these rarefied places
That only princesses can inhabit... Elsewhere.

It came to past that, as he was walking once more back
To this chamber in her soul,

He sensed the presence of the lightest,
... The slightest hint of a most elegant film,
... Of a veil.

She had, to ease his pain, spun a translucent diaphragm
That felt like the fluttering of a thousand butterflies on his face.

He instinctively stopped:
Knowing that the time had come for him to leave his space in her heart.
He had correctly trusted her:

Knowing that she would never have used the weight of things ugly
to part with him.

That veil, by the very fragility of its lace,
Needed only to imply what he needed to impose on his world:

His willingness to submit to the gentle,
Sanguine crucifixion of his heart:
Dividing forever his life between the before and the after.

*A Gothic tale of a vanished Princess*

# LA DOUCE PRINCESSE

Ils s'étaient rencontrés dans la riche et complexe douceur
Qui, des fois, peut s'épanouir dans le site entre la jeunesse et
l'âge.

Bien à l'abri, là, entre l'innocence curieuse et les souvenirs
inoubliables.

Chevalier dévoué et gardien de ses secrets, elle... lui avait permis
De la protéger de ses susceptibilités et de ses faiblesses.

Cachant les failles intimes dans cet être apparemment sans
failles,
Elle avait mis la sauvegarde de son bonheur entre ses mains.

Il se savait, quant à lui, hors de danger
Là... dans les espaces de son âme.

Car cette princesse lui avait réservé un endroit spécial:
Où qu'il se trouve à travers ce monde
Il pouvait toujours retourner chez lui.

Des étoffes en soie précieuse et des draps en coton d'Égypte
Guidaient ses pas le long du chemin
Et adoucissaient son effort vers ses courbes nuptiales.

La tiédeur de douces brises au-dessus de l'impressionnisme des près
Flottait au-dessus de ses yeux... dirigeant sa marche.

Des parfums faits des plus riches essences d'huiles exotiques
Annonçaient la proximité de sa présence.

Elle lui semblait faire partie de toutes les parties de la nature :
Grande prêtresse de muses sensuellement habillées,
Elle avait même provoquait des envies cachées dans le regard
des sages druides.

Elle était les pistils fertiles rougeâtres dans le jardin.
Les feuilles luisantes rassasiées après les pluies.

Le pulse des vaguelettes embrassant ses doigts
Effleurant le courant au-dessus de la rive de leur étang favori.

Elle était devenue l'incarnation de soupirs
Alors qu'il murmurait à travers le duvet de sa nuque
Sur l'arrière-plan d'une circulation européenne effrénée.

Elle était la voix et le nom si aisément reconnaissables
Parmi tous les autres, en tous lieux et toutes langues.

Il n'aurait pas été plus surpris de son omniprésence
Que de celle des étoiles, de la lune et du soleil

Elle était et avait été... toujours là.

Comme toutes vraies princesses dignes des droits de leur sang bleu,
Elle avait été dotée d'une générosité de cœur,
D'une grâce de tempérament et d'une sensibilité d'intelligence.

Elle lui fit donc, imperceptiblement, presque silencieusement, sentir
Que le moment de la libérer était arrivé.

Les princesses se doivent de vivre parmi ces espaces rares
Où seules savent résider les princesses... c'est-à-dire... ailleurs.

Il arriva qu'il retournait une fois de plus
Vers cette chambre douillée de son âme,

Il sentit la plus légère présence,
... le plus petit indice du plus élégant des films,
... d'un voile.

Elle avait, pour lui épargner la douleur, tissé un diaphragme translucide
Qu'il croyait être des milliers de papillons tournoyant autour de son visage.

Il s'arrêta instinctivement :
Percevant que le moment de son départ était arrivé et qu'il lui fallait laisser sa place dans son coeur.

Il avait eu raison de lui faire confiance:
Sachant qu'elle n'aurait jamais utilisé la laideur des choses pour
se séparer de lui.

À travers la fragilité de sa dentelle, ce voile...
N'avait eu qu'à insinuer l'obligation qui s'imposait maintenant
sur son univers :

Son accord tacite de se soumettre à la douce et sanglante
crucifixion de son cœur :
Divisant pour toujours son existence entre avant et après.

*Un conte gothique d'une princesse disparue.*

# RORSCHACH NATION

Looking in from the outside:
And this time it feels good.

Recent immigrant with increasing language skills,
And 'feeling his oats' ... in the new parlance.

A chance to be constructively critical
In this academic setting of thorny problems,

Of original intent
And parceling apparently biblical meaning to words on paper.

The culturally sharp comment is on his lips:
Aimed at deconstructing solid foundations
And the torpors of embedded political beliefs.

The professor glancing from across the lecture hall.
All the eyes of political science class looking toward the usually
quiet student.

The presence of that sassy blond from the dorm up the hill
Making the moment that much more self-defining.

This was his chance. Upper level class in his major.
Time to discuss complex obscure issues:
Federal law and the courts.

He is ready to pounce... He never did.

He was going to make this brilliant remark:

"Isn't looking for the original constitutional intent
Like looking at a Rorschach blot?
Everyone sees what he wants?"

He could not chance mispronouncing the main word
And made, instead, a bland observation.


*Gentle ironic criticism from immigrant*

# DREAM SEQUENCE 3: THE SILENT MAN

The bio-digital event had long ago happened:
Insertions of all kind of chips with all kind of purposes
In various parts of body parts.

Mankind and machines had long ago
Reached, taken and accepted that Faustian Oath and Bargain:
That of the incestuous cohabitation of things aware and unaware.

Speed and survival had dictated this willing self-invasion
In the name of efficiency and knowledge.

Thus, left in the dusty past were the cultural quirks of others:
The foods and entertainments from all over
Had been reprocessed, recombined, refined
Into an amalgam of apparently joyful flattened topographies.

Children and adults were taken to digital museums
To experience for the first time the weirdness of diversity:

In ancient anthropological scenes of the Twentieth First Century
When quaint people had been known
To eat and speak quaint things and languages.

That was before the advent of the world of... One language,
When that language had overwhelmed the hearts and minds of all.

He, man of some extremes... had decided one fatidic day,
To learn to read a yellowing text of poetry.

A text in that disintegrated tongue from one of his ancestors
Found on a cellulose binder of multi sheets
        ... Known as a book.

He was able to reconstruct the smoothness of the syntax
Not unlike symphony directors, through their musical intuition,

Reconstructed the intent and phraseology
Of Eighteenth Century composers from black dots on partitions.

He decided, henceforth, to Communicate in only the lost beauty of
that tongue.

Upon remaining stubbornly mute or misunderstood,
He was institutionalized until his self-mumbling death.

# OF REVOLUTIONS AND LUCK

A few thousand miles of cold Atlantic.
Haphazard crossing in creaky boats.

The Eighteenth Century had advanced political ideas
Much beyond its technology.

A few thousand miles of cold Atlantic
Gave the needed germination time
For blasphemous thoughts of non-monarchy:

Such chaotic beliefs as individual rights
And self-determination of future,

Led by political leaders intoxicated
With the fumes of liberty.

Giving this fledgling nationhood of North America
The critical benign time of incubation
For the evolution of revolution.

Relative calm, time and space that would not have been
If easily surrounded by the threatened monarchies of the time.

Instead, great emptiness of ocean and land
Was basically all this new world had.

It was... Basically... All it needed.

*Heard in Political Sciences discussion about the American Revolution: "The French Revolution didn't stand a chance: surrounded within miles of its borders by its philosophical enemies: other monarchies."*

# UNVARNISHED

A walk on the working docks of village fishing fleet
Transformed itself into an ultra-sensory glance
At the skeletal underpinning of things and people.

No artificial overlay. No idealization
- If not in the outsider's glance -

No posturing in the glistening biceps
- Except for the pure practicality of strength -

No beautification of apparatus and machinery
- Just some balancing baby shoes or simple Cross -

Indeed the metal of the vessels was gouged, pitted:
Seemingly allowed to rust to its innards and proud of it.

The planks of the docks grossly nailed and nailed again:
- As if into submission -

The original skin of their wood had been drained of all natural
appearance:
Deep striations giving them a colorless petrified look.

Under the watchful eyes of worried seagulls,
The shirtless dock workers were mechanically straining
Against the dead momentum of huge buckets of fish and ice.

But it could have been Egyptian stones or pink Tuscan bricks:
The gestures seemed mythological in their brute physical presence.

Muscles were battling against muscles
And were working among the banter and immediacy
Of the solidarity of a beer at the corner Italian club.

Seemingly no machine part was in its original state.
Adaptations of all sorts and quality kept the miracle of operation going.

Dependable and durable green tape. Metal bands and wooden wedges
Held barely recognizable apparatus in place.

There seemed to have been a pride in stripping things
Of their useless skins and jadedly showing off
Their essential essences found in the skeletal elementary.

The accidental interaction with these fishermen and their families
Dashed any misconceptions or attempts to intellectualize the setting.

There was an insular earthiness and purposeful saltiness in the
mannerism and language
That put me back in my place... Outside.

No time for some sort of elitist voyeurism:
The one found in the oils of museum paintings.

People and things were living their instants in the instant:
With no time for the luxury of reflection.


*Accidental walk on weathered fishing docks by a philosopher.*
*Or*
*The softness of ideas meets the marble of feeding your family.*

# FAUSTIAN THOUGHTS

Crystallized moments. Iced tears on salty residues of sweat.
Wrinkled sheets and shapeless globs of melted candle wax.

Tipped flowery Champagne flûtes and empty drippy bottles.
Half opened chocolates and half eaten fruits.
Drawn shades and strewn clothing.

All of it, unsuccessful attempts at grabbing handfuls of happiness.

Disorder under foot and at the foot of the bed.
Disorder in his life at the end of his life.

Shadowy reflections of hellish visions
In smoky mirrors of the future of his soul.

Sins and guilt clearly written in sanguine scratches
Seen on bare chest oval between ghostly paleness of opened silk shirt.

All of it, remnants of remnants that bring thoughts of inevitability
down to earth,
And making you look up languidly at strands of shredded innocence.

All the elements that make up elements
Of love of living... And fear of dying.

As the old philosopher sits in his petrified library,
Prisoner of his leather chair.

While no amount of smugness in his opulence,
No amount of physical and financial comfort,
Could satisfy his Cognac driven souvenirs.

As he thirsts helplessly for a molecule,
Any molecule of those moments...

Of dirt... Shame... And youth.

# LIVE TELEVISION FEED FROM *A* CRUCIFIXION

You would like to think
That such moments would have been rendered that much more
solemn and momentous.

You would like to think
That an informed opinion would have attacked the Roman action.

You would like to think
That knowing men and women would have been repulsed by the sight
Of such rash punishment for such mild words and thoughts

You would have thought...
     ... But you would have been probably wrong.

Spin doctors of the official decorum of Roman doctrine;
The nodding approval of slighted Jewish Rabbis in smoky temples;

The slightly under washed followers of a charismatic trouble maker;
Glassy eyed tired field workers going by the hilly site after a day of labor...
     ... All in disinterested torpor

In front of the molecular death of precious molecular humanity.
The redundancy of the event displaying prosaic images on burnt retinas.

Except for
     ... The personal, carnal or maternal tears

From the
     ... Very temporal pain of two women kissing the feet.


*Inspired by the advent of the overwhelming availability of information in the Internet era.*

*And the saying: "Le plus ça change...." [The more things change... the more they stay the same.]*

*Nota bene: the indefinite article in front of Crucifixion.*

## OPENED PORTAL: THOUGHTS OF SISYPHUS

Bewilderment acted as a giant emotional press
And crystallized grains of sand filtered out of the fine mesh,
Spreading into edgeless envies.

He instinctively, like a curious youngster,
Brought some of this powder to his lips to have a taste of yesterday.

It created an immediate excruciating burning sensation:
The one that every child rightly feels upon touching fire for the first time.

Like the inner corridors of ancient temples,
There are pieces of time that are reserved for the gods and their favorites.

Yesterday, we are sternly led to learn or believe, is for fantasies of the heart,
And, astrophysics, in its frigidity, seem to unravel in only one direction
... Away from it.

But that is not taking into account the masochistic level of pain
That the artist is willing to endure to achieve his goal:
... An agnostic leap of faith backward.

And so it is now with lips and soul indecently wide opened
That he swallows firry extracts of the distillates of moments past
To intoxicate his consciousness with the appeal of purified escape.

Time had come:
He felt an uncomfortable sensation, a visceral desire,
For what seemed to be an instinctive return to something.  Anything.

He became overwhelmed with this need for a primordial return:
A cyclical, yet beneficial menstrual action out of his control.

It felt splendidly natural and human by its cleansing, fruitful effects.

He longed for that maternal place that first suckled him with warm
visions of quietude:

Giving him tempting impressions that all things would be forever good and soft.

That place that existed in him. That should exist in all of us,
If we made ourselves emotionally, tactually, sensually available to things.

A place of illusionary yet tender happiness.

The philosophical equivalent of a reptilian flight reaction
From threatening philosophical dead ends:

Deadly Sisyphean emanations that escape from the boredom of the moment.

And so, he turned to those diminutive pieces of precious memories
Forgotten like school yard marbles carelessly left on the dusty planks of wooden shelves.

Moments and people doubly burnished but not erased
By the normal abrasion of time and the acidity of events.

Burnished to a sheen; but not erased... so that an afterglow of their presence could still be detected like an emotional Big Bang.

It was through his fervor...
... The blandness of the moment...
... And his disillusionment of the task at hand,

That an hallucinatory, alchemic and youthful spectacle offered itself.

Majestic date trees in a bluish humid Moroccan night
Hovered over naked light bulbs smoking in roasted lamb fumes.

Strong paternal hands guiding him through the sweet sour acrid smells of rancid oils.
The antithesis of refined bourgeois maternal cooking.

The whole experience flowering into a foretaste of what would be his fatal adult attraction,

That is... a taste, for the coarse, elementary nature...
Of things: Joyful. Youthful. Opaque. Slippery and sensual.

It caused him pangs of earthly guilt in his Catechism list of ethical
weights and volumes:
The moral. The proper. The venal. And mortal.

All the while producing in his mind an attractive display full of seductions.

A time portal must have opened itself...
... For he was now amidst the bluish dark fir trees bending their ice
covered branches of a brittle New England February.

These contradicting landscapes had been vying for space in the
clair-obscur of his heart all these many years.

Overlapping double ganger visions of layers of cultures fathering
strong winds blowing toward a setting full of violent and erratic
barometric pressures.

In both landscapes existed an intermingling of a vein pumping,
eternal and ever present adolescent vigor.
He could see himself kneeling near enigmatic feminine forms, with
bottomless eyes.

Sinuous shapes as extraordinary as the alphabets entries in their
exotic passports.
Figures defined by the intimate complexities of foreign mores.

Under the flapping greenish whiteness of bedroom sheets,
They had become his Olympias next to the pounding ocean of the
Setting Sun:

All these cultures, all these persons cross fertilizing and becoming one.

The oppressive heat of the last breath of the Sirocco from the Sahel
And the icy snow hitting his face had the effect of ritual cultural
blades... making him bleed.

The body and the mind are not made for these extremes.

There should be an extended time of adjustment... of transfer.
But the end is always too soon.

More acrid smells and more burning flesh of lamb meat
On coals from the corner stand next to the taxi stand:
...The bled and the snow... The bled and the snow.

All of this infernal heat among the swirls of puritanical whiteness in
the water crystals in his new world.

He had been expelled from a universe of warmth and obliged to
learn how to survive in streets where life was surrounded by the
apparent stillness of absence of heat.

Incredulously he whispered:
"These places unfortunately really exist in this world, don't they?"

Left behind was a world where things and life had the invisible
boundaries of the fickleness of desert sands:

The desert... that landscape that remains when all things are taken away:
The imposition of limitless visions.

The desert: that place that existed before playful gods decided
to control us with strings of restrictions and boulders of daily
responsibilities.

The translucence of the sheer cotton djellābas acting as pregnant
sails filtering the grains of sand.

It is right and good to think that this is how mankind evolved:
From the nonjudgmental chaos of primordial warm muds,
Then to the challenging one of the frozen tundra of daily life.

At every step, we can envision one of us looking around and asking
himself:

"What am I doing here?"
Scanning the emotional immobility of the stone hill above him.

Nature itself seemingly rejecting the humanity in his glance:
Making the desolation more desolate.

But once in a while, there must have been a moment of particular
honest revelation, maybe even of guilt, on the part of these gods:

Letting mankind get a glimpse, a real glimpse
Of the meaning of the dehydrated undercurrent of nothingness underneath.

In a weakened state, man felt a Genesis moment.
Then... turning to elements of life and living around him,
He savored such things as...
The rust of dust filtered sunsets
The shimmering surface of Summer lakes
The presence, maybe, of that woman...

And then, for safekeeping and remembrance,
He proceeded to bury ...
His fears
His questions
His passions
And his vaporous hopes...

Everything that had and would define him...
Into the landscape
And into her.

He then walked down the hill toward the nagging boulder: Resplendent
in its roundish volume...
And decided to start pushing again.

# UNIFIED THEORY

Inventions have risen out of needs: real or imagined.

Sitting next to a warm fire seemingly started
By magical lightning conquered cold nights.

Cleverly sharpened spears and rocks
Made for shorter meat gathering.

Uneatable furs and skins more useful on frozen human skins.

Mankind rose to the top of the pyramid:
Thus starting to think royal illusionary things
About itself on this whirling stone of earth.

Making sense of the now and hereafter inevitably came.
This realm was more susceptible to invisible envies and limits.

With often an astonishing relationship between the difficulty in the
belief and the passion in the following.

Smoke density. Cloud geometry. Bird singing.
Bleeding entrails and distant thunder:
Came to fill the voids left by the voids in men's heads.

We even diversified our gods:
Seeing them in streams... Gold... Or simply men.

And much well before Einstein's heavenly attempts... Even unified them
In the deserts of our religious meanderings.

To only go back every time to the minutia of interpretation
Of specks of details of the very meaning of meaning...

To better kill each other again.


*Not your father's Catechism*

# If*...

Since his earliest days of his early High School years
He had seen them, the culture, the language...
        ... On screens of his classrooms and his mind:

The pinkish stones of elegant Mansard roofs.
The melted sugar lace of church steeples.

The colonnes Morris with wild splashes in Toulouse-Lautrec colors.
The iconic double cones red signs guiding paved streets.
The jaded laziness of sidewalk cafés.

The crazed round about traffic and Romantic red tiled rooftops.
The self absorbed arched reflections of city bridges.
The competition for affection between large boulevards and medieval
alleys.

These and other images reinforced again and again
In Spartan black and white details of classic New Wave movies...

... With his first wide eyed introduction to that boyish haircut for women
That would remain etched forever on his soul
And appear finally and carnally across from him at Place Clichy.

But he came to fully... viscerally appreciate
The risky complexity of the ingredients of the French *conditionnel*...

... Upon leaving, that day... At the airport...
        ... Not having satisfied her personal feelings
                ... And thus... Condition.

He understood, now,
        How combining the future stem
                To an imperfect ending
                        Would lead to a compound with magical powers.

It could...
        In the arid Universe of grammar,
                Reconstruct the rich complexity of human emotions

And the fragility of human destinies.

Thus recreating the crisscrossing of opposite currents that are part of life.

Made of the future and the past,
      This luscious grammatical mood
            Became... no less than organic... As he walked away
from her.

Not having satisfied that first clause... If...

Resulting in her future presence in his arms...
      ... That would never be.

*\* See glossary under conditional.*

# WORDS MADE OF SILK

You are left wondering who... and in what language?
Where... and near what lake or mountain?
How... and with what trembling fingers?

With what tear filled eyes and what ethnicity?
Under what sort of Sun and African shade?
Over what cold haunting and empty wind swept moors?

Along what talcum white beach?
In what asphyxiating and lonely city apartment?
And on what food stained table?

Among which neighbor's crying babies?
And inquisitive friends or family glances?

Under what and any
of these extraneous, unrelated and noisy parts of life

Did she write the beginning and the end of everything?

"... I love you and always will."


*Inspired by the movie* Silk *where the Nineteenth Century French character
gets a love letter in Japanese and the universal traits of love.*

# A FUN GUY

Ready to go out at two in the morning:
Stale granular hamburgers with dryness bathed in liquid ketchup.

Incapable of maintaining silent in silent library or lecture hall.
Inconsistent in fitting his schedule into any schedule of any heart.

Madly insensitive to deep emotions.
His beelike jumping from topic to person
Flattening multidimensional conversations and infatuations.

Adept at Frisbee and cards. Late to class and life.
King of the bullshit session and baseball statistics.

Master of disguising his awareness of his easy effect
On both genders: A man's man and a girl's dream.

Walking into a party, he bathed into existence:
Like a Titan, he drew energy from the bodies.

A sloppy roommate with a knack for wet towels on bookshelves.
But likable and tolerable nevertheless.

Until that early morning appearance in the doorway.
Full of the mud and leaves of a late wet autumn.

White as a sheet and his impeccable silky hair in disarray:

"I wrecked my GM sports car. I almost died."
Nearly in a whisper... as though a solemn wedding vow.

He was never the same...
    ... We both existentially learned to live with the change.


*One night during college years*

# SAME STREET, DIFFERENT WORLDS

The same polite side glances at the prized dark meat.
The children in their Sunday cuteness asking why the bird had
only two legs.

The sister in law had once more kicked her husband
Over his attempt at an off color political statement.

It didn't take long for scatological comments about digestive issues
To bring an air of school yard humor in front of the stately grand
father clock.

The social stiffness of the early part of the meal
Had dissolved in the wavy alcoholic vapors of chardonnay grapes,

Giving way to uncontrollable laughter,
Leading to more incongruous answers to misunderstood questions.

Complaints about co-workers and late nights at the office.
Spouses and their weird household habits.

Bad trips to Pittsburgh and lost luggage.
Impending birth and slipped disks.
Compliments on the sauce and smacking of lips on the pies.

All had been as it should be for a Thanksgiving:
Any Thanksgiving worthy of the name.

We had our world.
       While unknown to us,
               In our neighbor's... His wife was dying in his arms.


*Family tragedies and holidays.*

# IT WAS NOT BECAUSE SHE WAS GONE

It was not because she was gone:
No... She was still that fragile silver reflection
On the bathroom window of a full moon.

It was not because he did not think of her:
She was again the one mentioned in the pounding beat of a past hit.

It was not because he could not touch her any longer:
She was still the soft cotton curves on the sheets of warm summer nights.

It was not because he had no more to say:
He was afraid his friends would hear his thoughts in a noisy bar.

It was not because he could no longer ingest her fragrance:
That last date had the same Mediterranean taste.

It was only that she filled his vacant soul
By the solidity of her absence.

## OF BEASTS AND MEN

He had splendidly taken over the office desk:
Walking defiantly past the computer keyboard.

He had had these old man mannerisms:
Insisting on sleeping in the most inappropriate places possible.

He had a malformation of the jaw:
Leading to tuna enhanced flurries of flying food.

He was clueless of his place in the hierarchy of the animal kingdom:
Attacking with unequal results any night prowlers.

He had a predilection for sniffing steel belted tires:
Seemingly getting high on them.

In true cat fashion he came to you in his own disdainful way...

... All this adding to the communicative sadness
Upon closing contently his eyes into slits
While gently and approvingly sniffing her fingers

    ... One last time.

*"These stupid animals make me cry all the time."*

# DREAM SEQUENCE 4: THE LOST MAN OF MANKIND

Things were out of balance. The ends could not hold.
The rip, the gap had to filled and stabilized.

A human unit was out there: they knew it.
They had heard of it.

No built in controls and no aims.
       No particular purpose or known ability.
           Horror of horrors... No connectivity!

A potential disease for the body politic and social.
No parameters of morality and no baseline of mores.

No way to know what questions and insinuations could ferment.
What sort of demands and philosophical aggressions
Would he inflict on the hierarchy of beliefs and laws.

What sort of chaos could he bring to the homogenized soup
Of the accepted events and decisions of history.

Somewhere in a wet cave of some hilly backcountry was a man
Completely and dangerously disconnected to the world.

Freely thinking wondrous, incredible, unrestricted opinions
About himself and others.

Surrounded by the warm earth tones
Of the mud of murals on the rock walls.

*Imagining a future world and the search for a man who somehow had been taken out of the maternity ward without his biometric implant and set out, with his parent's blessing and hopes, into nature and freedom as an adult.*

*Also thoughts of the movie* Fahrenheit 451.

## MAGICAL INK

He would finger them once in a while:
These books with compressed memories.

Onion skin sheets, light as Italian cherubim:
He felt the need to slam them shut:
Thus keeping the memories intact.

Side notes, Metro tickets and wrinkled street addresses:
All solid witnesses against the daily voids of the calendar.

These gifts meant for the intellect:
Now precious talismans for the heart.

He had resigned himself long ago,
Among all these offerings,
To some certain realities outside of the universe of words...

... Why it had always been so viscerally difficult
For some of mankind, to built precious temples and icons
That would be believingly equal to their symbolic value.

He had received these human tablets from her... Mere carnal hands,
And still, watched them increase in value on his walls:
With no artifice, no smoky candles or chants.

Turning these common wooden shelves into a tabernacle
That are what tabernacles are all about:
The religion of what we crave... And yet, will never possess.


*"The last one reading this can shelve the book."*

# THE DESERT

Recurring visions of disembodied anonymous other hands,
Other lips... Tortured his sleepless thoughts.

Like sadistically pushing with the tip of one's tongue
Against the infected bubble of puss along the gum line,
He would replay her missing presence in someone else's
embrace.

It was upon rereading that passage from his past
That he caught himself in the truly absurd personal world
Of unattainable human longing:

That of envying the protagonist losing his wife's carnal passion
To the eternal seductive immobility of the immortal desert:

Giving him the emotional satisfaction of losing
To an incredible foe... Worthy of her limitless lubricity.


*"Then, with unbearable gentleness, the water of the night began to fill Janine, drowned the cold, rose gradually from the hidden core of her being and overflowed in wave after wave, rising up even to her mouth full of moans. The next moment, the whole sky stretched out over her, fallen on her back on the cold earth." From Albert Camus* 'The Adulterous wife'.

# LITERARY THEORIES AT THE PERSONAL LEVEL

Late afternoon. Late Fall Semester.
Upper level class. At upper level floor.

Hissing of old steam radiator.
And wheezing of venerable professor.

Thoughts turn to delicacies on dormitory menu.
Ten page paper on obscure islands in geopolitical dispute.

Details come to life on yellowed university note book pages:
Who he was then and the people in between.

Esoteric lecture of the molecular level of language and communication:
What we say. How we say it.
What we mean. What others say we mean.

The concept and the specific. The idealized word and the examples of it:
Stranded in the geometry of different personal experiences.

The very human need to capture our lives
Through inventoried and alphabetized words.

Our need to label the realities in our minds... and in our arms.

Symbolic, intimate, personal signs added in pencil in the margins:
Doodles in the interspaces of dreamy immediate romantic longings.

He had more than once lost himself
In the convoluted architecture of structuralism.

Then... the revelation:
The organic, pulsating and sanguine revelation.

The sign, The signifier. The signified.
All brought into a carnal whole.

The generic of... woman... had, since then, been seared into his heart
and mind

By the rich layers of her sighs,
The exotic of the settings,
The jewels of the moments
And... the infinity of her glance.


*Variation on the dry and removed concepts we learn in our studies and their seemingly real life intersection with our existence. Such as: the sign, the signifier and the signified from structural literary theory.*

## CLASSROOM

He had been looking for that tricolor clip for years:
Recurrently... religiously...
      ... Every year when presenting French holidays.

It had been safely sleeping:
In the far back right corner of the center drawer,

Having refrained from pulling it completely out:
One of the rollers was missing.

A particularly funny cartoon of himself,
      From properly scolded... talented student
          -Lovingly folded under a stack of notes- reappeared.

A wrinkled photo proof for an article in the fuzzy past
slipped out of a random folder 'logically' entitled: recipes.

He had returned the venerable desk to its empty state:
The one in which he had found it...
      Not unlike his classroom skills...
          These many years ago.

A clean slate for the next teacher he thought:
That's the right thing to do.

He had been tempted to leave a note of encouragement
      There... inside... in the middle... of that pesky drawer
      ... for the first minutes of class.

No... Too personal...
      Too distracting... Too sappy... Too pretentious:
          What would he say to encapsulate thirty years anyway?

One last look...
      He realized that he had been sitting with the lights off.

The custodian in the hall had just locked his door...
      For the night for him...
          For always... for the teacher.

# CHAPTER III

# POEMS OF NEW ENGLAND ISOLATION

Poems of New England isolation: Less connection with things and people. The mirror is often the starting point of ideas.

# DREAM SEQUENCE 5: THE PAINTING

Awareness of sweaty panic:
Standing on creaky floor board of his cold studio.

Silhouetted phantoms of easels somberly looking down.

A cottony light filtering through a prudish curtain on the wall:
He practically ripped the cloth aside...
The vision reappeared.

He had kept this canvass cleverly and prudishly hidden
Under the generic calm of a landscape.

Trying to imprison and appease unspeakable passions
Under layers of pretty watercolors living in a sleepy two
dimensional world.

But, infinitesimal cracks had come to the surface of the
paint and into his mind:

Among the sedate prairie green of the landscape
Had now escaped needles of light radiating like curtains in his studio:
Seemingly razor sharp brightness that made the darkness darker.

A self-sustaining energy started to melt the pigments of organic greens
And slowly, temptingly... like a burlesque stage
The landscape gave way to the sinuous intensity of a reclining nude.

A milky carnality inundated all the corners of the room.

A presence whose very volume hurt his glance from
trying to capture it all at once:
"Like the first time... Like the very first time"... he whispered.

He remembered having reconstructed her... from mere black shading
of charcoal sketches

But her image had inescapably seared his lonely soul:
His thoughts... eventually ending as thoughts of
precise paint onto the canvass.

Dreams of colors.  Sighs and hues... in varied nuances of life.
Screams of vermilions streaked into lightest touches of pink.

All from burning memory... late in the void of insomnia.

---

He realized that she had not belonged to his eyes only
Since well before the paint had dried.

Art had transcended intimacy and privacy
The instant that she had languorously leaned back
With her porcelain arms behind her head
And her thighs hinting at hidden happiness.

Layers of flesh colored splendors had escaped ownership.
The pliability of the cherished folds were at the beginning and end
Where things evaporate into carnal perfume.

An Odalisque pose on his poor bohemian bed
Magically turned into an Arabian translucence
With a surprising greenish metallic sheen in the cotton fibers.

And he had no right to deny this joy to the Other
As he had tried to deny it to himself for those many years.

He ran his finger tips on the paint:
The way one would barely skim the lips of a sleepy satiated lover.

Feeling guilt in a fertile hazy state:
The one between bottomless sleep and frantic creativity.

The uncontrolled mind and body instinctively measuring
The eternal truth of Things:
Beautiful and untouchable.

And then... In a quasi-religious prise de conscience:
The awareness of his cowardly lack of belief in his art...
        His own art.

He took down the curtain:

Letting his passionate gaze rest... There...
Where all passions eventually and rightly should
live...
In the work of art.

# THE FLOWER AND THE BUTTERFLY

She had arrived in his life under the double sign
Of the flower and its butterfly:
Black silk wings and heart of crimson pollen.

They formed a unique perfect union,
In days in his life when the center would not hold.

Instead of simple ornaments of summer afternoons
They had, by their symbiotic powdery existences,
Given solidity to the vaporous...
Meaning to the ephemeral.

A linkage between the ideal and the concrete.
The sensual and the untouchable.
Between void and belief...
Gaze and blindness.

In a mind filled with sharp edged realities of escaping grains of sand,
They... By the simplicity of their sun drenched matting dance,
The organic innocent simplicity of it,

Somehow gave... Purpose among meaningless spinning:

All of it protected by kisses between the Flower and the Butterfly...
The Flower and the Butterfly.


*Of philosophy in the backyard.*

# EVAPORATED THOUGHTS

Frantic searching for scraps of paper... any paper:
Discarded cheap news print before its demise,
Some with remaining oily food stains.

Train schedules with columns of random stops.
Sunday inserts of shouting headlines for consumer overload.

Anything and everything possible
That would last the eternity of a reading.

Families hoarding yellowing letters of old soldiers to loved ones.
Touching references to time and places, people and circumstances
On the back of now precious picture postcards.

On living room walls, in makeshift tabernacles of respect,
All the remaining books, on all and any topics, neatly lined up:

Revered and gently stroked by admiring friends
Like so much vintage wines and flags of cultural wealth.

It gave to late night fellowship gatherings the feel
Of mankind's early transmission of folklore and history.

Cross fertilization of oral and written communication
That would have taken place around the village elders:

Taking place now in glass and stainless frigidity.

Lest the past... its wisdom and madness...
        Its beauty and genocides...
                Would remain dissipated as orphaned electrons.


*The after effects of massive solar winds on the erasing of all the world's digital storage.*

# FRAGILE LETTERS

Curved scrapings into the bark of the biggest plane tree
Will lose the shape of precious names with every season.

The same as names written with strong reeds of Camargue
In the wet sands of the indigo Mediterranean:

Giving these fragile letters their tender arrogance.

All these attempts are no more than messages in a bottle,
Thrown into the future unknown,

Hoping that they will be read by the knowing fingertips,
Made of the flesh of our flesh...

Who will recognize in the remaining wavy folds
The remnants of our loving protective presence for you.


*Thoughts on First Grand Child*

# UN COEUR EN HIVER

Wandering the emotionally vast expanse between the stove and
morning coffee...
A messianic voyage in an emotional desert away from people and goals,
Filled the voids with stupor... calm and continuity.

Traveling the most merciless of spaces...
The ones of the very awareness of empty spaces.

Carnal warmth had become the powdery stuff of early morning
fireplaces:
Cooled embers: dying remnants of those rare first moments,
All natural offspring of pregnant first glances.

He and his heart had gradually come to rest...
Seated here... on the margin of the joyful heartbeats of things.

"A heart in winter", he thought hearing his wrinkled lips whisper...
As he settled for a lonely spiritual hibernation.

And then... this intrusion of a chance reality...
An apparition quickly absorbed into the stringy fibers of his
personal needs.

The frost of isolation gave way to the steamy balm of recovered
memories:
Numbed parts of his heart...
The parts where she had breathed...
Woke up from an arid unconscious state.

She had reappeared: trailing golden threads of possibilities and...
impossibilities.

A thaw started... first unbeknown to his flesh
And then under its own impulse.

He had found, once more, the rich dangerous chaos inherent in the
rich landscape of envies and the living,

Where once had only existed
Stupor... calm and continuity.


*Loosely inspired by* A Heart in Winter"("*Un coeur en hiver*")
*Directed by Claude Sautet*

## REMAINING TIME

Pieces of conversations and involuntary eavesdropping:
      Drone of plastic canned music and muffled wallpaper sound

Forced social intimacy with fellow patients with imperfect bodies.
      Nondescript waiting room styling and fishing magazines.

Requisite quasi sunset paintings and masculine sail boat racing.
      Unsuccessful attempt at avoiding other unsuccessful other glances.

This antechamber to the gate of the proverbial future;
      This Green room for the rehearsal of yet unwritten acts.

Nervous tic in trying to look comfortable on sadistic chairs.
      Spying from the corner of sight for any hints in nurse's eyes.

When... in the middle of a merciful stupor we hear our name:
      "... The result of your biopsy is in..."

*In the doctor's waiting room*

# STEADY HANDS

Bar stool to the extreme right.
Sport bar in three-sport city.

A quiet place to decompress.
To burn away the anxiety with a cheap whiskey.

Continuous echoes of excellent news from the surgeon...

Giving the walk from hospital to that stool
The feel of a prison break.

But some game was over and talk turned to...
... The hands.

These five fingers had no equal.
The nerves, the tendons and the nervous system attached to
them...
Quasi godly.

Their steadiness under pressure
Proof of sport royalty.

Worth every multiple thousands of dollars per hour.

While on the extreme right side
The silent father was trying to set an emotional price
On this anonymous surgeon's hands...

Which had gently... professionally... and assuredly
Moved major abdominal organs to save a life.

# ADDICTED TO THE DREAM

Void and hunger in his blood.
Gaunt look of drug alley survivor.

Licking upper lip with white sickly tongue of hours of fevers.
Nights of hallucination.

Disappearing presences and frustrating nightmares,
Shrouded in perfumed sinuous lace,
Gently intoxicating his better conscience.

Plump rounded flesh of easy carnal satisfaction lost in luggage of time.
Warm tactile hedonism soaked in the cold sweats of immediate
reciprocal joy...
All killed by the dirty needles of reality and time.

Dirty streets of the concrete of harsh choices and harsher decisions
Leaving him on this one way street to hellish lonely isolation amidst
the uncaring crowds.

Visceral starvation at the cellular level of the soul.
Every last organic shred of his being crying out for that fix...

That flesh... Whose minute presence by its very proximity
could satisfy all things.

Left instead with uncontrollable daily yearning:
Shaking hands.  Mirror... and the visual salvation of the mask of the
shaving cream.

Aimless shuffle to the car.
Mechanical reach for the office phone.
Inattention to random voices.

Laws of man and time having perverted her once iconic nature.
Her very glance declared an illicit substance
Prohibited by everything and everyone.

Guilty and condemned to live in the dream ever since.

# FLATTENED MEMORIES

The disorder of the room had the lineage of dignity of birth:
Born, as it was, from the disdain for the materiality of life.

The unaffected solidity of her spirit imprinted into the
hardness of objects...
Remnants of events... steadfast witnesses to her unweaving spirituality.

Memories, made of the jagged edged mosaic of what is repeatedly
The hardest of the darkest side of humanity:
Its inhumanity.

World Wars smearing the warmth of a child's innocence
With the slippery sheen of precious coal clumps
Picked up in the gulleys of early morning streets.

No heat... and even less hope for a dying mother
Whose vaporous image of sweaty consumption
Would henceforth define the unattainable.

Wayward aerial bombardment:
Flack, of modernized killing machinery, falling all around.

Single minded attempt to protect children
With preposterous yet touching absurdity
Of the overturned protection of bistro table.

Destiny, on that morning, showing a soft spot
And subtle appreciation of the gratuity of survival:
By leaving behind a chunk of smoking metal
In the shape of Corsica at their feet.

Family cat showing its unsolicited humanity
With gift of a large piece of precious, stolen Roquefort.

Contrasting reaction from well fed family members
Refusing to hand out... handouts, to cousins.

Once priceless official looking letters

Of arbitrary travel and dislocation,
Lifesaving certificates of passage and entry.

Odysseys of the body and heart:
Leaving both disillusioned.

Packing the breath and width of these physical remains
into flattened boxes:

Her thoughts of temporal humility, eternal divine nuptials:
Pure bride in the hermetic stones of convents.

Choosing instead conventional life in the sewage of the overflow of reality.

The unexplained and unexplainable survivals such as
The much too young
Crystal blue eyed soldier looking down at his machine gun
Once too many time.

———————————————————

She seemingly wanted to safely encase the limpidity of these memories
Away from the harsh rays of neglect.

There... safely between the four walls of her last non-descript hours.

The blank flatness of the paint must have collaborated
In the replaying of gigantic visions...

Those of various people
Of... Courage, generosity...
Jealousy and treachery.

The very volume of things and deeds.

Deeds and things forcefully
Willed by the forceful will of her.

Things and deeds
Imposed on her in cascades of impositions:
      Political. Parental and intimate.

All of them coming to rest in the eternal rest from life
To be summarily compressed into unappreciative receptacles
Of wrinkled skins of papers... cold in front of their frigid future

Minutiae of moments in various states of her special categorization
Of her own secret Dewey System:
With folds within folds of varied obscure hierarchy and
importance...
Placed upon angles of protrusion from folios and stacks.

All without exception having been personally and lovingly
Abandoned to their quiet corner of well-deserved sleep.

All these pieces of time past having given by their very presence,
A few feet away on their shelf of retirement,
A link to a sleepy television filled present.

A Classic painterly touch to the disorder of this room.
A surprising dignity...sign of a natural formality of the soul,

Akin to classical paintings of precious oils
Made to extract... to tease, with the apparent ease of a master's touch,
Pearls of salty tears on the cheeks of widows.

All of this... In a background...
        Of... Courage, generosity...
              Jealousy and treachery,

Remnants of which were carried as deep sighs in her surviving
family's lungs:

To be released in billowing rainbow of crystals in a sadden
December sky.

*Clearing out the living quarters of a deceased person whose life was touched by
the major conflicts of the Twentieth Century.*

*To the music of "Douce France" by Charles Trénet.*

# LITANIES FOR THE DEVIL

Some have made him a rejected angel. A fallen pretty face.
Mankind's feeble attempt at the transliteration of godly speak.

Beautiful virile beast full of the attraction of purity of belief.
Overflowing with visceral, sensual zealotry,
As seen in the eyes of adoring crowds at demented mass
gatherings.

We also show him full of angst and jealousy.
Relegated to the bowls of some horrid world.

Full of torment and tormenters.
An evil Yin to a good Yang.

Evil... attributed to dysfunctions of the mind,
Marginal behaviors by marginal beings.
Consequences of vicious vapors of the blood.

Properly depicted and carved into paints and stone
On walls of cathedrals and retold in morality plays to children.

Encased into the somber corners of our centuries.
Entered between the slimy book pages of history.
Hidden behind acrid cleansing priestly incense.

All these visions... all these attempts
To more safely solidify Him and his cohorts.

All these representations to put him in a place:
In order to better know his place.

All these projections away from us,
To project him on the walls of our fears:

As though he could exist without us... and outside of us.

But not unlike a greasy substance picked up on the bottom of soles,
Try as we might we cannot shake it off.

And try as we might... in the generous image of Doctor Drieux of the Plague,
It was never meant to be shaken it off.

It will live in the horrible eternity of the images of the day's news:

We try to comprehend the disemboweled gaze of African women
Or the self-righteousness of inquisitorial fires.

They will continue to haunt us
As some perverted beautification of evil.

All this debris of the mind and heart keeping us awake
And feverishly thirsty at night. Existentially replaying our guilt on our soul,

And so, we return to our bed... passing in the darkness...

Our sleeping children.

## CAFFEINE FOR THE SOUL

Sleeping... would have been fine.
Nothing... would have been plenty to do.

Mindless viewing of mindless television plots
Would have remained stimulating.

Contemplating the emotional voids of the overfilled Mall boutiques
Would have added merciful useless knowledge
To wanting sections of brain.

Like layers of dull pigmented paint
Drying in the stale air of a musty basement...

Things and ideas... people and memories,
Plans and dead ends... life and living,
Building and planning... destroying and regluing,

All these pieces that we like to undervalue, overvalue,
Ignore and embrace,

All these many and varied variable of moments
Following other faceless moments...
Had come to a majestic grinding halt.

A perfect paralysis at all the corners of the emotional compass
Had set in.
Affirmative and negative had lost their definition:
Due to personal lack of interest in either one of them...

And then... unexpectedly... like that telephone call for a dead man walking...
She hit enter... and her name appeared on the screen...


*Existential moment: Engaging the future in the world of modern technology.*

# TRYING TO TOUCH INFINITY

*A poet's asymptote*

A concept. Manipulation of signs.
Parallel worlds of unfeeling pluses and minuses.

Lines that sinuously rush toward each other
Tentatively trying to brush one another's curvatures.

The calculus of the heart never far behind
In its frustration of things close yet so far.

The sensation of things envied... Yet denied.
Things within reach of each other's thirsty molecules of flesh.

Lines that seem to sense the other's presence.
Distance somehow rendered infinitesimal:

More intimate with travel and time.

Somewhere in this universe of arbitrary laws,
Of correct and wrong, of isolated sections and subsections,

Exist invisible laws against nature and instinct
Toward things and people wanting to touch and not pretend.

It was her music. Her restaurant and similarly bizarre food.
The same overlook and ragged rocks.
The same miniscule bridge and dangerous road:

Replays of shared happiness.
Now simply beads of sweat... He thought... Hers.

## SILK SCARF

Organic birth gave the silk scarf
The soul of remembrance.

This precious substance
Had known the intimate joys of her warmth.

Having conformed to all her demands
In sinuous symbols of lubricity,
It had spread itself modestly to prepare the moment.

And after all was said... After all was done,
The magic cloth kept in its fibers
Traces of her name as wrinkles of imperceptibility.

# THE IMPORTANCE OF INSIGNIFICANCE: A FABLE

While capturing their infinitesimal part of the sun's warmth,
Some delusionary crystals thought themselves at the center of
their deluded world.

Quaintly thinking that they were imposing their existence on the
solar presence,
While in their glorious bath full of melting beads of essences...
Of things dependable and eternal.

Each pretentious crystal feeling at ease with its pretentious status.

Meanwhile, other unhappy crystals wallowed in their anticipated
crystalline mortality:
Understanding the ephemeral nature of their sheen
In the figure of the mortal solar symbol.

And so... in the brittle Lilliputian world of...
Ambitions and despair,
Self-aggrandizement and self-deprecation,

They were all meaninglessly correct... and equally wrong.
None of them having any impact on the snow bank.

Except that... once in an elegant while...
One of them could encompass in his mind
The whole of that void.

Envision in his sight... the majestic inescapable spectacle
Of that collective whole... that mound of snow.

A momentary sentence, a fragmented phrase,
The sparkle of the consciousness of presence.

Then passing it on...
        In that glance on an oil canvass... that score of noble music
                That turn of a gentle verse... That generous
gratuitous gesture.

Could it be that knowing some of the rules of the endgame
And seeing some of the strings of the Universe
Is all the significance we can ever hope to achieve?


*Learning the role of being insignificant upon watching the collective sparkles of sunlight reflections in the innumerable melting crystals of a snow bank.*

# MAJORELLE BLUE

*Marrakech fantasy*

She lives where he had left her:
Shimmering folds of blue silk and hints of rounded flesh.

A translucent milky pearl amidst the patina of fire treated mosaic stones.

Fire and flesh. Presence and longing.
Plasticity of life and the immobility of the statuesque.

His senses turn off and reality becomes just a slit of light filtered by
eyelashes:
He feels his mind wavering...

What part is of the past? And what can still be touched and savored?

———————————————

Desert and ice. Snow and scorpions,
That have learned to coexist in his soul all these years.

All this time away from this Maghreban beach.
Away from the too luxuriant and luxurious youth.

The unwelcomed knowledge of years
And its consciousness of the drought of age.

Ah! To be in the time resentful emptiness of the bleds of the Maghreb
And to be able to conceive solely of a fluid world full of tomorrows.

Of a time when the past had yet to be constructed...
And did not... yet... matter.

She is still seating... in that photograph,
In that place of many facets... an offspring full of sensations that
only the innocent glance of youth can engender.

A vision akin to Cézanne's imposing the quaint childlike immediacy
of flattened perspectives:

Where fervor of the gaze transcends the cold logic of the Universe.

She is still that resplendent reflection of...
Understated fire, virility and femininity.

A place full of hedonistic ambiguity and exoticism
Where the norms want to be aggressively mounted and transgressed.

A place in this magic blue garden on the other side of this brave wall
Separating the puritanical desert sands from the rich inner earthly
nourishments...

A place where wisdom is found peacefully sleeping in the tepid shadows.

---

From the West, through the lace of white stone arches,
Enters a hint of ocean blue:
The greenish ocean blue creating an echo of contrasting nuances.

A rhapsody of colors in the key of Majorelle blue
Overlays itself and creates a vibration of collisions
Of shades of blues against blues.

To the East, the dryness of the limpid blue of the Atlas sky
Is violently penetrated by the gray angles of the mountain passes.

Marrakech... where the past magically had always learned to cohabit
with the present.

Where beauty had the stately elegance of these privileged places:
Places where beauty does not need the artifice of imposition.

A place where beauty existed well before knowing its name... art.

Not far from Marrakech where sensuality had casually wrapped
itself in sheer white cotton:
Long before it knew of the restraints imposed on voyeurism.

Not far from Marrakech... lives this walled garden
Hidden by the fertile shade of pregnant date trees.

A shy Maghreban mirage made of sandy construct:
A desert of grainy fantasy.

Sharp silicon pieces that acted the part of no nonsense
fortunetellers:
Telling adults the tales of the pain of paradise lost.

These grains of truth gently inflicting stigmata of unwelcomed
wisdom on the open skin.

Tattooed reminders to the eyes of what the heart had lost
Upon leaving behind this space whose echoes had followed him
To the cold shores of the Labrador.

*Inspired by* "The Girl in the Silk Dress" *in* Clair-obscur of the Soul.
*"... Surrounded by the beautiful Maghrebin murals,*
*A translucent porcelain seated amid the turquoise mosaic.*
*A pearl, color of the very milk of fertility.*
*Exotic voyeurism of the surroundings*
*Explodes in his soul with no guilt.*
*Pardoned by the natural beauty of this vision*
*Which has found in this setting of protected privileged shivers,*
*The symbol of her gift of true quasi-virginal voluptuousness."...*

*And*

"Femmes d'Alger dans leur appartement" *by Delacroix and* "La fille aux yeux
d'or" *by Honoré de Balzac.*

## THE END OF THINGS

On the other side of the remaining fragments of stars
There... over there...
Where a weakening star light still pierces nothingness,

In some fore lone corner of everything
That had ever been and hoped:

Nothingness will replace consciousness of impending void.

All will have been said and done. Destroyed and rebuilt.
All for the enjoyment of temporal joy. All for the illusion of tomorrows.

All for the solidarity in the recognition of the elegance of solidarity:
If not its victory.

And then... like all well written tragedies,
At the piercing end of dramatic pain between stage left and right...

There... at the intersection of existential moments,

We will once more know... since its first inception in our soul...
What it is... To want and not have.
To have and to lose.

To love with fullness of heart and emptiness of embrace.

Then... in a noble... very human gesture,
In the elegance of just a human glance,

Things will cool off and be gone
To that dark place that has scared all little children
Since their first concept of being orphaned by their loved ones...
... On that distant day.

---

These thoughts had come to his mind as he reflected on the
crystalline winter night sky.

He then returned to the harsher... intimate reality
Of knowing that she...

Like that beneficial nuclear heat... would also never come back.


*Inspired by a science documentary about the end of star energy in this universe.*

*"... It is under the half empty sheets that we curl up and swallow hard...*
*...and make noises similar to choking... gasping for air...*
*...not the guttural noises of lubricity...*
*...but those similar to the trashing of imminent death...*
*... And so the world comes to an end... on tear-spotted sheets and droplets of love.*
*The last efforts are a mixture of grimaces and smiles...*
*...tears amid ecstasy...*
*...and the awareness... the physical awareness... that every motion is the last one...."*

"And so the world comes to an end" *in* Clair-Obscur of the Soul.

# FEAR IN THE SOUL

Something natural, disfigured into the perverted.
Transforming the pleasurable into disgust.

Images of inspiration
Only to soil them with viciously arid thoughts.

Ripping the heart out of beauty and installing in its stead
The emptiness of hopeless emptiness:

Somewhere... Sometimes... In the misery of the artist...
In a silent kitchen full of the early hours of dawn
This distortion of the normal has permeated
The sinuously shy vapors of coffee.

It is conquered in some painful and surprised future
 As art and life take back their share of the living.

While that fear is filed away on some upper shelf
 Always unsteady and apt to fall.

Those moments of emotionally arthritic shooting pain
 Upon approaching the piano keys...
As she closes the door.

The incapacitating trembling
Of the paint brush between the thumb and index...
As the sun is setting.

The nauseating revulsion in the studio
Upon looking at a marvelously pregnant piece of marble...
As the model wraps herself against the cold.

The abject panic invading the sterility of the soul of the artist
 Upon catching a glimpse of what should be... Must be...
Precious inspirational moments of magic
Waiting to be encapsulated by the art of the artist.

Left now... In search of the return
Of that instant of explosive genesis.

That contact... Between sight and beauty.
Sense and imagery... Touch and abandonment.


*Trying to write for days....*

# OF ZEBRAS AND MACHINE GUNS

*Kenyan fantasy*

Regal postures of well-fed lions under merciful shade.
Regal symbols of afternoon tea under white colonial drapes.

Living colors of impeccable pretentious green lawns.
Alignments of fragile fruit trees with trunks of white wash
In an ocean of burnt yellow hues of tall grass.

Quaint attempts at awkward implantation of starched collars
And white cocktail dresses flowing in orchestral romantic winds

Busy servants.  Imported tableware.
Civil behavior. Civilized setting.
Watchful eyes of nannies for wayward serpents

But no indigenous danger and calamity could rival
The carnage of youthful soldiers dying willingly
For crown, country and certitude

In the muddy fields of Europe.


*Upon watching a movie taking place in Kenya during World War One.*

# CONFESSIONS OF A EUROCENTRIC

*Love letter to America*

Makes you long for the bad old days when...
In the smoky darkness of movie houses
... Europe felt a twinge of jealousy toward you.

Rebel Without a Cause. Teenage characters fighting out of boredom
With the by-products of accumulation.

James Dean in immaculate tee-shirt akin to Roman breastplate.
Crashing of cars the size of a Paris apartment kitchen.

This New World... bigger and faster.
Easier and cheaper.
Magically renewable.

Full of space for the soul and gaze of the lonely cowboy.
All seemingly more colorful and wider through Cinemascope.

Could buildings be that tall
And cities that artificially organic?

Its tourist in Paris full of swagger
And strong money in his pocket:

Apt to sweep away any Hepburn
In a single voyage on the Seine.

Nothing was too dear to buy or too deep to find.
Hollywood could capture the presence of anything:

The back alleys of Casablanca and the Coliseum of Rome
All in perfect realistic replicas.

Greatness often doesn't feel its ankles in the reality of the unsustainable,
With its head so high in the vapors made for divinities

Unfortunately... films have an ending.

*America 2011*

# THE SYMBOL OF THINGS GOOD

It is a moment when we profess our creed:
That the child is... indeed, the best link in the best of worlds.

He is the symbol of the strength of Good
That surprises us in the fragility of birth.

He is the light in the darkness
Contradicting some of the pages of history.

His presence, full of futures, melts the obstacles to the fullness
of human happiness...
... Man-made and otherwise.

He is the bundle of reconciliation of Things and People
Representing the emotional and lasting sheen
In the diversity of the mosaic of life.

He will remain, in the warm protective glance of those
Who have lovingly, carefully and emotionally swaddled him.


*To my grandson.*

# AFRICAN HARMONY

May the man-made calculus of evil stifle itself
In a jungle of meandering dead ends.

Equations of multiple geopolitical knowns and unknowns
Hiding behind the ultimate human sin...
       The volition to kill.

Damn evolution!
The elephants of Africa should have taken over!

Let them... by their majestically non Machiavellian thinking
Cleanse the savannahs of the blood stains near the overturned
camp fires

May they nobly turn their heavy bodies
Toward the humid clouds to the West,

Ponderously walking toward the green vastness
Quenched by the cyclical rains.

Let the hyenas offer the smoky breath of the birth of their young
To early morning mist over their den.

May the pregnant sunrays of Spring
Wake up in a song of streaks of gold the flocks of merciless birds
of prey.

In the brittle shrubs, a microcosm of eternal battles
Between scorpions and spiders erupt.

Let the lion and the crocodile kill for their respective meals,
And then... Let them all rest with the clear conscience
Granted by their lack of consciousness of evil.

Not far... The elephant trail snakes into the acrid fumes
Of burnt thatch roofs and overturned evening meals.

As the younger elephants approach, protected by the herd,

The dying cries of dying tribes filter through the weeds.

The scene reflected in the tender bulbous eyes of the regal beasts,
Looking toward the melting foggy hills.

*Reflection on the scene from the movie* Michael Clayton *when the main character has approached a group of horses quietly standing on top of misty morning hill. The scene shows a lawyer who has sold his soul, silently and near tears, looking into the eyes of these majestically gentle beasts. The viewer feels an attempt to transfer, to communicate human anguish unto these animals.*

*And... The obscene dichotomy of the beauty of the African continent and its continuing human misery.*

# ETERNALLY...

Did you know that he wakes up grasping wrinkled sheets in the
shape of her curves?...
... Refuses to get up in order to breath in longer the last vapors of
her presence?

That he lives in a world of miraculous calendars and time pieces...
... Of shifting birthdays and eternal youth?

Did you know that he drinks his coffee next to the door...
... To be the first to see her enter once more?

That he will confuse in a magical flower garden in an urban street...
... The smells of petals and that of her flesh?

That he will embrace ghosts in the darken nuptial shades...
... As he holds the vinyl dryness of a steering wheel?

Did you know that his cosmopolitan soul
Will feel ridiculous as his tears dilute what was her favorite ethnic
dish?

Did you know that he will turn his head repeatedly
To possess one more time the fleeting glance of a similar glance?

Did you know that he will be the last to realize
That she will never appear again...
... Until his next sleepless night?

# MAGICAL DUST

She fluttered in... Riding the warm breezes of endless fancy:
Black wings and red patches.

She landed on wrinkled folders of inattention,
Fanning valiantly the stagnant air of routine.

She had the quivering beauty of things desired and fragile.
Gentle and firm. Immediate yet illusive.

She opened herself on the open cover of an abused folder:
Offering him the intimate view and a privileged foretaste
Of her slender curves.

In a hopeless battle, the folders were folded,
The briefcase in hand... and the locks unlocked.

He found himself in the luxuriant world of cravings:
Where multiple realities satisfy human needs.

Visions of things done and touched.
Of wishes expressed and granted.

Of things easy and too easy.
Of cottony warmth and firm flesh.

Low hanging fruits of earthly Paradise.
Deep sighs of satiated temptations.

Coming back to consciousness...
He was fingering butterfly powder,

Leaving behind streaks of memories
On the humid side of his cheeks.

He felt the frantic blood flow in his temples:
Wondering whether this magical animal had ever existed.

*"... He realizes today... that it is this animal... ephemeral and fragile*
*Like its powdery beauty...*
*...it is she... who would survive him...*
*...and she... who will offer to those... passing his tomb...*
*...the blushing images of passion, which she had witnessed...*
*This same passion, which will burn her black wings,*
*Still moistened by their love.*
*...this beautiful animal, full of nervous silence,*
*Will land on the puddles of salty corporal nectar...*
*...she will die batting her wings which...*
*...with natural grace and without anguish...*
*...will declare... gently...*
*...that they have loved each other.*
*"I want to kiss you all over... and over again..."*

*From* "Black Butterfly" *in* Clair-Obscur of the Soul

# GLOSSARY

This glossary of words, names and terms is added for the convenience of readers to enhance their enjoyment of and access to the full range of language and meaning used in the poems. Many of Jean-Yves Solinga's poems are translations from French and are littered with words of particular cultural and literary reference from this language. There are also religious and historical references and other terms which may be unfamiliar to some readers. The briefest definition or explanation is provided only to support the meaning in the poem. Of course alternative definitions exist and these can be found in any good dictionary, thesaurus or encyclopedia. This glossary of words is presented in alphabetical order to avoid the need to repeat those that appear in more than one poem.

**Asymptote**: A term used in calculus to describe a line or limit that a curve approaches but never touches.

**Bled**: The country side, the fields, the landscape in Moroccan Arabic.

**Brel, Jacques**: A Belgian singer-songwriter. Brel composed and recorded his songs almost exclusively in French, although he recorded a number of songs in Dutch.

**Camus, Albert**: An agnostic writer and moralist of the Absurd. A philosophy where man confronts his consciousness of the meaninglessness of life. Best known for *The Stranger* whose main character exemplifies the consciousness of the Absurd. Camus is part of a long line of moralists who try to deal with good and evil in their vision of a godless universe.

**Clair-obscur**: Light and darkness. French name for Chiaroscuro in Italian. Painting technique of strong contrasting light and shadow effects on the canvas. [nota bene: no 'e' at the end of obscur in French]

**Conditional** [Conditionnel]: In French, a supposition can be written with the Conditional mood [i.e. le conditionnel]. It is constructed with the future stem of the verb, to which is attached the imperfect past ending [i.e. l'imparfait]. Thus the poem treats lyrically this grammatical intersection of future unknown.

**Couchon, Alain** : French composer and singer of anti-war song "C'est comme vous voulez."

**Delacroix**: see "Les Femmes d'Alger."

**Djellābas**: Flowing smocks or robes usually of light white cotton worn in North Africa.

**Docteur Rieux**: character in Albert Camus' "The Plague." In it, Camus, a humanist and an Atheist, describes the loneliness of a man fighting the scourge of the disease in spite of the odds against him.

"**Douce France:**" iconic song by Charles Trénet that captures his lyrical love for his land.

**Existentialism**: A philosophy championed by Sartre according to which one defines himself by, and is responsible for, his own actions. I do, therefore I am.

**Honoré de Balzac**: Prolific French Nineteenth writer. In "La fille aux yeux d'or" This classic étude of the Parisian underworld from Balzac's History was considered shocking in its day. The story still provides a jolt of naturalistic cruelty, orientalism, emotional detachment, and paradoxical twist. It is as much a portrait of Parisian manners of the mid-19th century as a study of one man's infatuation with a woman of impossible beauty and innocence. The story describes an erotic servitude concealed behind the walls of one of the finest mansions. When Henri de Marsay, the pampered and decadent heir of Lord Dudley, is led blindfolded to an assignation with the woman he most covets, he finds that his hated rival is his true brother—or, rather, sister—in vice. [Excerpted from *Amazon.com* by Regina Marler.]

**Ionesco, Eugène**: French playwright of the Theatre of the Absurd. He was the master of using the stage to question, redefine and study the elements in language and communication. "The Bald Soprano" was one of his early successes and presents some of the iconic figures and themes of the Theatre of the Absurd. In this instance of complete disconnect, the aforementioned The Bald Soprano does not appear and cannot even be mentioned.

**"La fille aux yeux d'or"** : see Honoré de Balzac.

**"La revenante"**: Translated as "The ghost" has a slightly different connotation in French in which it can often imply the coming back of someone dearly loved in his or her life time (i.e. a cherished family member or partner)

**"Les femmes d'Alger"** : Painting by Delacroix showing the setting of a harem in full romantic colors and style.

**Lilliputian**: A term derived from *Gulliver's Travels* (1726) by Jonathan Swift (1726), which is set in an imaginary country of tiny inhabitants. Therefore, anything that is extremely small; tiny; diminutive can be described as Lilliputian.

**Machiavellian**: This refers to being or acting in accordance with the principles of government analyzed in Niccolò Machiavelli's *The Prince,* in which political expediency is placed above morality and the use of craft and deceit to maintain the authority and carry out the policies of a ruler is described.

**Maghreb, Maghreban**: Setting Sun: in Arabic, the Maghreb [in particular Morocco].

**Majorelle blue**: named after the French artist Jacques Majorelle. An intense purplish blue found in Moroccan mosaic tiles.

**Majorelle, Jacques**: Born in 1886 in Nancy (France). In 1919 he settles in Marrakech to continue his career of painter, where he acquires a ground which was going to become the Majorelle Garden. In 1980 Pierre Bergé and Yves Saint Laurent repurchased the garden and restored it.

**New critic**: See Signifier

**"Olympia"**: In this text it is the painting by Édouard Manet. Powerful artistic statement of a reclining nude by the artist.

**Rockwellian**: An idealized view of American life as depicted in the many paintings of Norman Rockwell.

**Sahel**: Large swath of land including the Sahara desert.

**Scribal corruption**: Textual errors made by transcribing, translating or generally misreading the original text leading to misinterpretation of important beliefs and seminal religious concepts.

**Signifier, signified**: The linguistic sign is the union of the signifier (a collection of sounds that distinguishes this sign from others) and the signified (a concept or meaning arbitrarily and conventionally assigned to this collection of sounds). Note that the signified exists only in the head of a language user. [From Wikipedia]

**Sisyphus**: Character of Greek Mythology condemned to endlessly push a boulder up a hill. Taken as an example by the French writer Albert Camus as a symbol of mankind's condition.

**Theater of the Absurd**: Theater in which playwrights like Becket, Adamov or Ionesco, would deconstruct on the stage what is meant by communication, words, meaning: characters with the same name; pantomime; proliferation of object to project meaning; senseless non-linear dialogs; etc...

**Tin Tin**: popular comic trip detective with his ever faithful dog, Milou, at his side.

**Trénet, Charles** : Iconic velvety singer of great French classics of the World War Two years. He captured his lyrical vision of French culture, Paris and human sentiments.

**Truffaut**: "Fahrenheit 451." Seminal movie by the French director of a world where books and the knowledge they impart is prohibited.

"**Un coeur en hiver**": French film by Claude Sautet. A talented violinist falls in love with the owner of a workshop that repairs instruments. Stéphane is incapable of reciprocating any emotion toward the beautiful woman.

**Voltaire**: François-Marie Arouet, French philosopher of the late eighteenth century. Best known for Candide. Attacked hypocrisy and religious intolerance. Promoted civil liberties and religious freedom.

# INDEX OF TITLES AND FIRST LINES

Titles are in bold, and the first lines are in regular text.

# ABOUT THE AUTHOR

**Jean-Yves Solinga**

Jean-Yves was born in Algeria, to French parents, but at no more than a month old was traveling to Salé, just South of Sidi Moussa, in Morocco, where his father, a gendarme, was posted. The family settled and Jean-Yves spent an idyllic childhood in the sun of North Africa. He attended French grammar and secondary schools. His memories of that time are of the joy of being aware of the pleasure of sight; the cocoon of the innocence of youth unconscious of geopolitical matters.

His family, having decided to settle in America, sent Jean-Yves, at age 14, ahead alone in order not to miss the start of the school term. Living in New England he would experience first hand one of his many future encounters with the freezing cold and snow which up to that time had been seen on Christmas cards.

He had already written poetry by the time of his bachelor's degree and a brief tour of duty in the US Army after which he began a career teaching French Language, Culture and Literature in Connecticut schools and colleges. He completed a Masters and then a PhD on North Africa before retiring in 2004 at which time he earnestly concentrated on his writing.

Jean-Yves has written four full length volumes of poetry published by Little Red Tree: *Clair-Obscur of the Soul* (2008), *Clair-Obscur de l'âme* (2008), *In the Shade of a Flower* (2009) and *Landscape of Envies* (2010).

# LITTLE RED TREE PUBLISHING

Little Red Tree Publishing, established in 2006 by Michael Linnard and Tamara Martin is based in New London, CT. Taking as their motto "delight, entertain and educate," they strive to combine their love of quality books with an interest in fiction, non-fiction, poetry, music, art, design, history and photography. From the start they defined themselves, consistent with the finest traditions of small independent publishing, as preserving and expanding the dwindling opportunities for previously unknown poets and established poets to publish a full collection of poetry. They passionately believe that well crafted books and accessible poetry should be celebrated and presented as such with conviction and confidence. Therefore, all books are coffee table size, 7" by 10" or above – an emphatic statement of intent and a celebration of the poetry. Little Red Tree is named after a Japanese Maple (Acer Palmatum), planted in 2005, and both still thrive. Below is a selection from the 32 books published since 2006.

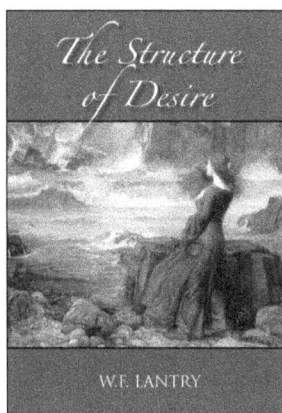

*The Structure of Desire*
by W.F. Lantry

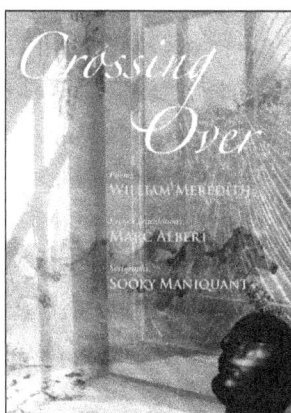

*Crossing Over*
by William Meredith

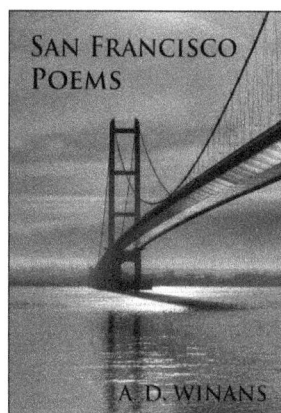

*San Francisco Poems*
by A.D. Winans

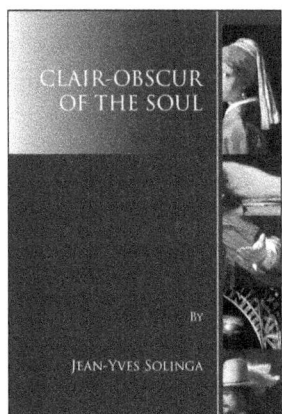

*Clair-Obscur of the Soul*
by Jean-Yves Solinga

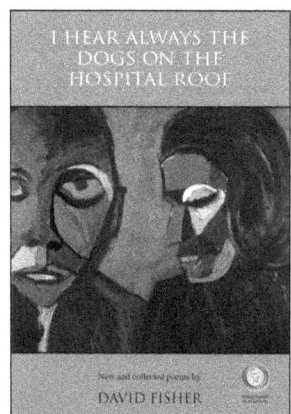

*I Hear Always the Dogs on the Hospital Roof*
by David Fisher

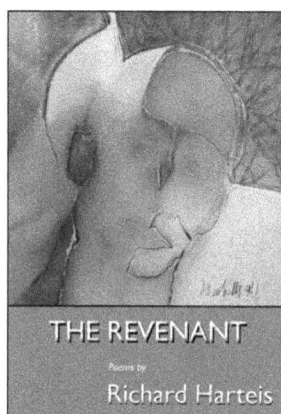

*The Revenant*
by Richard Harteis